Management Consulting's Black Box

Mike Provitera & Mostafa Sayyadi

Copyright © July 7, 2023, Dr. Michael Provitera, Motivational Leadership Training, Fort Myers, Florida USA

All rights reserved. No part of this publication may be reproduced, distributed, or transmitted in any form or by any means, including photocopying, recording, or other electronic or mechanical methods, without the prior written permission of Dr. Michael Provitera, except in the case of brief quotations embodied in critical reviews and certain other noncommercial uses permitted by copyright law.

For permission requests, write to Dr. Michael Provitera @ **docprov@msn.com**, with the subject title addressed "Attention: Permissions Coordinator," and visit **http://docprov.com** for free workbooks found in his business book section.

ISBN: 9798366670166 (Paperback)
ISBN: To Be Announced in November 2022 (E-book)

Library of Congress Control Number: 1796

Any references to historical events, real people, or real places are used fictitiously. Names, characters, and places are products of the author's imagination unless otherwise documented.
Front cover image created by Mostafa Sayyadi
Interior book designed by Dr. Michael Provitera
Line-by-Line Editing by Dr. Michael Provitera
Printed by Motivational Leadership Training, Inc., in the United States of America. Website: **http://docprov.com/hire-mike.html**
For Management Consulting Contact Dr. Mike's administrative assistant at 954-226-0340.

Contents

Foreword
Introduction
Preface
Chapter 1: The Art of Management Consulting in the 21st Century
<u>How To Assess Your Training Skills</u>
Chapter 2: Building a Foundation of Cultural Cohesiveness
Chapter 3: Expanding the Management Consultant's Black Box
Chapter 4: Becoming a Transformational Leadership Consultant
Chapter 5: Becoming an Authentic Leadership Development Consultant
Chapter 6: Serving Clients as a Management Consultant
Chapter 7: Building a Transactional Leadership Consulting Practice
Chapter 8: Building A Culture That Thrives
Chapter 9: The Right Corporate Structure Formula
Chapter 10: How to Succeed in Strategy Consulting
Chapter 11: Becoming a Knowledge Management Consultant
Chapter 12: Managing Risk Requires a Knowledge-Based Approach
Chapter 13: A New Path to Organizational Knowledge Management
Chapter 14: Emerging Technologies and Knowledge-based Companies
Chapter 15: Driving Diversity, Equity and Inclusion
Chapter 16: Talent Management: The New Norm
References

Dedication

This book is dedicated to my two daughters, Janet and Lauren, as they both begin college together. Wishing them enjoyable and interesting studies as they grow and learn.
I also want to dedicate this book to my girlfriend Jean. Jean is an amazing woman, and she is the most generous and good-hearted woman. Her father Joseph, let him rest in peace, and her mother Angelina did a wonderful job raising her to be the most beautiful woman in the world---inside and out!

Foreword

By Mateo Gomez, M.B.A., Miami, Florida, USA

Many words are a result of management consulting: Administration. Operations. Supervision. Leadership, and Supervision, to name a few. Words that all relate to management consulting. Words that sound controlling. Words that all relate to credibility, intelligence, and order as organizations, and people, build their brand. Words, such as the ones above, are certainly talked about in an MBA class, but what relevance do they truly have to your career? First, and foremost, they are words that automatically create a power structure in your mind. Second, Leadership and Management are two words that could be used almost interchangeably. However, they are not necessarily the same. It is important to remember, though, that to have effective management, you need a good leader or a good group of leaders. Let me take you through my thought process behind my thinking – one based on logic and ideas, and the other based upon my own personal experience. As professionals, we all might start at the bottom, trying to become the best person that we can in our company, and eventually get to that management position that that bachelor's or master's degree helped us ascertain. But just because we got to that management position, that does not mean that we are leaders. It is important to remember that even though a title might promise us a position or at least a promotion, it does not mean that we learn all the skills needed in order to be effective. Then how do you learn those skills that will build our personal brand? One way is to listen carefully and critically think. Your knowledge is comprehensive and began when you were five years old. At that time, we listened to the people around us. Now, it is important to listen (and read) about theories and models of management that are effective. Learn from other leaders, your co-workers, and your customers. But most importantly, listen to your thoughts and feelings because this builds your authentic leadership presence.

Let me explain. I am not a huge feelings person, but this is when you actually need to listen to what is inside you. Why be in a management position if the group you work with does not enjoy going to work or they do not want to talk to you? Remember when that was you that did not want to go to work to deal with those folks in management positions? Or remember when they spoke to you in code? You probably what they meant but you felt that you were alienated. Thus, my personal view is to learn from your experience.

We have all been there. We have been that student, that professor, that teacher, or that mentor to others. We have been that person starting fresh in that entry-level job, but we have also managed others. Learn from when you were that student and see what worked and did not work for you. Know the difference between what should stay in theory-form and what should actually be applied. Simply listen to what you feel deep inside.

What about the other skills? Here is another tip – be grateful. Thank the people around you. Thank the ones that are there when fires need to be extinguished. Thank your team. Thank the ones that taught you what you know and got you to the place that you are. Thank the ones giving you feedback. Even thank the ones that you feel don't appreciate what you do. This keeps us humble. It helps us remember that we need others to get us to where we need to be. We need others to help us exceed and be those leaders that we were meant to be. It helps us to remember that we are not only the substance of that degree hanging on the wall or the job title that we have. We are humans and we need other humans. It helps us remember that we are replaceable and that anyone can take our position. Thus, we need to be grateful.

As a leader, you have your list of tips and tricks. Attributes that you tallied up about what you liked and did not like when you worked for someone. Use those as milestones on how you should be in your leadership position. That is the greatest tip I can give you. Before there is any professional consulting done, listen to yourself and be grateful for that knowledge and the people that taught you what you know.

Remember to return the favor. Be that mentor. Be the one that gives feedback and help others get to where they want to go. Be a consultant to anyone that knocks on your door and wants your opinion on something or is seeking advice. Be a "person" to them and don't talk to them as a computer. Be that trustworthy person and be that mentor and leader that every successful person has once had. Make that person you work with want to come to work and want to learn. Be that educator and teacher of what is right and wrong. Be that leader in that management position that is a role model for others to follow.

Management does not have to be a hierarchy triangle. It might be like that on paper or to the HR department, but don't let it feel like that during your day-to-day work with your team. Now that you have my tips on leading yourself and others, you are ready to make that profound changes that you will learn in Dr. Michael Provitera's book "Management Consultant's Black Box." I wish I read this book when I was studying management consulting in my MBA program. It is a practical appellation of management and leadership concepts. Easy to apply to oneself and one's organization as they add to their consulting competencies or begin a new career as a management consulting. I hope that you enjoy this book as much as I do. I often refer to the book before meetings and when I meet with clients. I strongly recommend that you continue reading and make this book one of your references to your successful management career.

·

Introduction

By Mike Provitera

For many years I have told people that although there are a lot of books on leadership, there is only one that serious aspiring leaders should read---*Transformational Leadership*, by Bernard Bass. According to a leading university, Michigan State University, most scholars credit the concept of transformational leadership to James MacGregor Burns, a political science and leadership researcher, who in the 1970s, defined the actions of transformational leadership as "when one or more persons engage with others in such a way that leaders and followers raise one another to higher levels of motivation and morality." However, in 1985, Bass, a leadership researcher and professor at Binghamton University, expanded on the ideas of Burns to develop the Bass Transformational Leadership Theory, consisting of four main components of transformational leadership in the newly developed mode. Most recent books on leadership have been about how to lead people through challenging and tumultuous times, the post-pandemic recovery, and what organizations must do to create the new face of leadership. These books are filled with a plethora of seemingly practical applications about how to handle the new normal and what needs to change. Yet few penetrate deeper insight into what makes a great leader. By contrast, Bass offered a buzzword with credence, clear water survival, through transparency, equity, and inclusion. He says that the true leader potential is not in the ability to delegate but to serve in an authentic way. The choice to be authentic comes with the territory. It is not a mindset, it is not an emotion, it is a realistic viewpoint that involves the whole person—warts and all.

This, too, is a book that any management consultants or leaders who are serious about making a profound impact on change will have to be read. The Management Consulting Black Box builds directly upon Bass's framework and then expands to include knowledge management with a deep understanding of the followers.

For Bass, being a leader emphasized the capacity to lead with charisma. Only the leader can have the necessary charisma to lead while followers nod their head in agreement. In some cases, charismatic leadership created the black hat of leadership with a darker side. It was not Bass's intention to create the charismatic mindset of leaders in a negative way, but nature of greed and con artists brought out the Enron and Bernard Madoffs of this world. Bass did add the necessary foundation that both practitioners and scholars needed at the time. He expressed the formula for success in a way that was not captured by writers and researchers of leadership up until that time. This movement led to the leadership work of many scholars such as Burns, Hersey, Blanchard, Avolio, Stogdill,

Yukl, George, and Luthans.

The challenging economic conditions and global competition increased tenfold in one year (2020 to 2021). Large corporations acted proactively by responding to the demands of customers, clients, and suppliers. Leadership development plays a critical role in business and fundamentally affects the way corporate functions run. When looking at leadership from a new perspective, management consultants not only should be aware of leadership models but should also place more emphasis on applying what works best for companies in the current work environment, and most importantly, what does not work. In many cases, management consultants must inform executives what not to do, and ask them to remember to question themselves in the way leadership scholars train executives by opening the training platform with "Who would want to be led by you?"

Thus, the key for every management consultant is to select yourself as your own client and make an appointment with yourself. Develop your own authentic leadership, have a story to tell, tell it well, and improve your talent by reading this book. Now!

Preface

By Mostafa Sayyadi

The evidence from recent studies suggests that authentic leadership can enhance organizations to achieve sustainable change and a higher degree of effectiveness. In fact, when executives embrace authentic leadership, the organization sees increased revenues and better satisfaction by employees and customers.

Management consultants realize that they can play a critical role in developing authentic leaders.

Servant leadership has also been touted, in some circles, as tantamount to executive success. Novel insights into how management consultants can help organizations enable interactions and provide more effective solutions to solve organizational problems.

Hosting the continuous influx of company-wide experts to share their knowledge may be underestimated and underutilized in a post-pandemic world. This book exposes the critical role of management consultancy which allows a rich basis to understanding the mechanisms by which knowledge management and operations risk is influenced.

Insufficient consideration of the impact of management consultancy on the effectiveness of knowledge management has been exposed and we attempt to address this concern.

Management consultants address culture, strategy, and structure from a new mindset today to enhance decision-making during the post-Covid-19 pandemic. Building on the three aspects of company culture (collaboration, trust, and learning), organizations attempt to continuously innovate and create new and valuable services and products through applying new ideas and knowledge.

Thus, the aim of this book presents beneficial managerial implications for management consultants. Particularly, this book indicates that management consultants can build a suitable workplace for better implementing corporate strategy through facilitating the four strategic dimensions of analysis, pro-activeness, defensiveness, and futurity. We suggest that management consultants make the effective changes that are posited in the four dimensions of corporate strategy.

The scope of this book is enhanced, nurtured, and exploiting social capital to keep the culture together and build upon the foundation that helps organizations prosper. This book will offer novel insights into what management consultants can take from social capital theory to build social capital by affecting structure, culture, strategy, inter-company networks, and stakeholder orientation. Practical guidelines for management consultants provide a more effective facilitation of social capital in their client's companies.

This book is prefaced by the emerging technologies

that have been on the rise since the pandemic due to the large platforms of remote use. Knowledge management is the key that makes technology an integral part of business success in the post-pandemic world.

I found myself deep in the heart of quarantine only to find that management consulting is more important now then it was before the pandemic began. I got together with my partner, Dr. Mike Provitera, and we created this book for you to build a profitable business for yourself and watch your life soar!

Chapter 1

The Art of Management Consulting in the 21st Century

The post-pandemic corporate world has better-managed desk space, right-sizing is an ongoing concern, workweeks have been restructured, and there is a strong talent-age-gap, as many seasoned executives decide to retire. There is only one thing certain and that is that change is inevitable.

Leaders are reshaping many things. Three aspects that draw management consultants to the table are organizational culture, organizational structure, and technological advances. These three tenets are changing the way we manage knowledge in organizations. The C-Suite, wherever that suite may be, is the focal point for finding the right remote-working formula for the post-pandemic. This weight is on their shoulders and management consultants can help them.

Here are some nuts and bolts to consider as you conduct your management consulting practice.

Show up with a **Technology** mindset. In the post-pandemic environment, innovative approaches help an organization's survival. Technological advances coupled with knowledge-based initiatives enhance survival. An organization's technological capabilities allow it to leverage knowledge in a more efficient manner by using electronic meeting software platforms as a necessary medium for success. Management consultants address how technology, when easily adaptable, provides a chance for survival in the post pandemic world.

Management consultants are using Zoom, WebEx, and internal communication systems to reach a broad-based training platform. We found minor limitations to this type of delivery platform. For example, hackers attempt to break into sessions, people fail to mute or have distractions when speaking, and individually home-sponsored internet connections may lack feasibility.

Next, have a broad-spectrum overview of the **Corporate Culture.** In a post-pandemic world, culture has shifted from facetime to real-time and organizational culture adapted accordingly. Knowledge management and culture will improve communication among remote workers when it is used adequately (Balogun & Jenkins, 2003). When consulting, the key is to broaden the mindset to ensure that remote worker knowledge is acquired, not only from you as trainer, but also, through learning from others. This posits that tacit knowledge may become a strategic factor of competitive advantage when consultants can bridge the gap of post pandemic prowess to confirmed application of leadership and management skill competency. Thus, positively influencing competitive advantage through developing shared assumptions and values, which may manifest as tacit knowledge at first, as it is embedded in remote workers, but then is transpires to innovation and creativity as people apply what they learn. According to Van de Ven (1986), "Innovation is defined as the development and implementation of new ideas by people who over time engage in transactions with others within an institutional order." Thus, corporate culture could be enhanced by focusing on four basic factors, which are, new ideas, people, transactions, and institutional context.

We build our work in industrial/organizational psychology to develop the construct of executive job demands; discuss its major determinants; propose some of its key implications for strategic choices and leadership behaviors; and propose the usefulness of this construct in advancing research on numerous fronts, including agency theory, executive compensation, and upper echelons.

A key to management consulting success is based on sharing best practices and experiences which plays a crucial role. For instance, research posits that "Executive jobs vary widely in the difficulty they pose for their incumbents, yet research on top executives and strategic decision making has largely ignored this reality (Hambrick, Finkelstein, and Mooney, 2005). Many participants, during training, express negative connotations toward their leaders and we must acknowledge their point of view, validate their feelings, and then move on as quickly as possible. Thus, embedding knowledge in members and supporting this strategic asset adds as an internal marketing pull strategy that ignites the consultant-client relationship. Organizations are thriving to become a knowledge think-tank that competitors, customers, and talent are drawn to. The post-pandemic era features a learning culture as a precursor for knowledge creation (Huber,

1991; Garvin, 1993; Provitera & Sayyadi, 2022).

When training, time is of the essence. The executives we work with have proclaimed that they transmit information simultaneously and disseminate information in real time. Meetings, based on this philosophy, are quick, exact, and important, or they are deemed unnecessary and a waste of valuable time.

When delivering the actual training session, focus on the **Corporate Structure**. When we trained the executives at the City of North Miami, in Miami, Florida, we created a structure that addressed culture from a shotgun approach. Each training was designed the same way but each discussion, question, and break out group had different objectives and application.

We integrated the vast knowledge of each participant and their department, which created competitive advantage. Hierarchy, while still maintained and respected, gave way to a more general response system by subordinates. Followers felt as if they gained wings, learned to fly, and became much more gregarious during trainings. The decentralized structure that facilitated the exchange of ideas and the implementation of more innovative solutions was tantamount to success. While some people decided not to opine in front of others, by stipulating the power of decision-making in and around the organization, gave people a sense of empowerment.

We found that scholarly research matters when training. However, it must come across naturally. For example, trainers inspire participants to transform aggregate human capital into social capital to implement the required changes at the workplace after the training. When training in a highly formalized structure, we found much bureaucracy, and, in fact, we noted that executives themselves were perceived somewhat negatively, and they lacked the ability to contribute to the effectiveness of leadership in changing existing situations and in creating a better environment (Jung, Wu & Chow, 2008). Thus, in the post-pandemic, decentralized structures may improve interactions and create more knowledge in organizations while enhancing the management consulting capacity to deliver powerful training sessions.

The delegation of decision-making power not only creates a climate that develops inter-departmental communication within organizations but also sets a parameter for training cohesiveness (Damanpour, 1991; Woodman, Sawyer & Griffin, 1993; Sivadas & Dwyer, 2000; Cardinal, 2001, Provitera & Sayyadi, 2022).

The After Army Review, created by Todd Henshaw, Senior Fellow, Center for Leadership and Change Management, The Wharton School, and former Director of Military Leadership at West Point.

The After Army Review (AMR) is called "one of the most successful organizational learning methods yet devised," (Henshaw, 2021). It was developed by the United States Army in the 1970s to help its soldiers learn from both their mistakes and achievements. Since then, many companies have used the AAR for performance assessment. And yet, as Peter Senge notes, efforts to bring the practice into corporate culture most often fail because "again and again, people reduce the practice of AARs to a sterile technique."

The process itself is an active discussion centered around four key questions:

What did we intend to accomplish (what was our strategy)?
What did we do (how did we execute relative to our strategy)?
Why did it happen that way (why was there a difference between strategy and execution)?
What will we do to adapt our strategy or refine our execution for a better outcome OR how do we repeat our success?

The AAR is not merely an opportunity to focus on team performance, but also serves as a catalyst for cultural change. To set the stage for effective AARs, leaders must first create a climate of transparency, selflessness, and candor where team members can challenge current ways of thinking and performing. Everyone — leaders included — must openly share where their own performance may have contributed to a team failure and acknowledge the people and practices that helped create the team's success. Used regularly to assess successful and unsuccessful events, AARs will strengthen teams and improve performance, and can become ingrained into the DNA of the organization. When key learnings from AARs are shared, the experiences of one team can benefit the entire organization (adapted from Henshaw, 2021).

CONCLUSION

Management Consulting ---- like the rising prices in the housing market, the high demand for used automobiles ---- is in demand today and will continue to progress as a leading profession well into the future. As of September 29, 2021, management consulting employees in the United States in 2022 will be 1,941,883. Employment growth in this sector in 2022 is 4.8%, and the annualized employment growth from 2017 to 2027 is expected to be 5.1% (IBIS World, Where Knowledge is Power, September 29, 2021).

Management Consultants are in demand to help executives improve technological infrastructures, stimulate a culture of learning and collaboration, and provide the necessary human resources to flatten organizational structures. Thus, three vital areas that are in demand today and will continue well into the future are cultivating an effective culture, developing more decentralized structures, and building technological infrastructures that are void of cyber warfare.

Before reading on, take the survey on the next page and check your ability and status of management consulting.

Are You A Great Trainer?
How To Assess Your Training Skills

Michael J. Provitera

Mostafa Sayyadi

How Do I Rate Myself as a Trainer) has been published in HR Future Magazine (December 2022 Issue)?

This training survey is based on Jules Henri Fayol. Henri Fayol felt that every organization requires leadership. [1] [2] [3] [4] This statement suggests the universality of leadership. Thus, a trainer of leadership development must also be a practitioner to be able to train appropriately. In some cases, proper schooling coupled with consulting may suffice, but it is always good to have direct experience that relates to the subject when training. The third way to start a training career is to have direct experience and success as a trainer. [5] [6] [7] This survey will identify your capacity to train based on the author's twenty years of teaching and training executives.

Leadership ability becomes more important as a person moves up in the hierarchy. [8] [9] Thus, when training executives, managers, and supervisors, more emphasis on interpersonal and conceptual skills is the best way to engage leaders for success. While technical skills are important, and an emphasis should be made to show the participant's aptitude in their profession, leadership training expands this thinking to go beyond the technical abilities that are less essential for upper-level leaders. Keep in mind that there is nothing that is written in stone here, this is a judgement call based on training experience by the authors, and this survey acts as a guide, not an absolute transformation of the trainer's ability. Just as in addressing a gap-analysis before developing a training platform, this is a personal assessment of trainer capacity to succeed in engaging leaders for success.

Instructions: Recall your training capacity as you conduct or plan to begin a situation in which you are planning a training platform, opening a training consulting practice, or become a university professor or adjunct instructor. Now, it is the time to assess your ability to effectively run this training session. Fourteen areas will be assessed coming from the Management Historian Henri Fayol. Henri was one of the first to provide a formal style of management and leadership. You will test your actual behavior in each of the fourteen areas above. For each question, rate yourself according to the following scale. Insert your score form one of the following five options for each of the statements that follow.

5 - Like me
4 - Probably like me
3 - Neither like me nor not like me, perhaps undecided
2 - Probably not like me
1 - Not like me

How Do I Rate Myself as a Trainer?

Section 1: Division of work

1. _____ I try to follow the timed and planned modules while delivering the seminar.

2. _____ I try to develop an understanding of the timing and different steps needed to cover the material in a timely manner while addressing questions and answering them as the training evolves.

3. _____ I evaluated different ideas and ways of presenting the topic along with added exercises and videos and open up opportunities to add new in vogue material to the seminar.

4. _____ I have a clear sense of the participant's priorities in taking the seminar and helping them apply the skills to accomplish their tasks.

5. _____ I make sure the clients that hire me are informed about the degree of progress in the training seminar.

6. _____ I am open to alternatives when they arise during training if it would help engage participants.

7. _____ I adapt the sequence of training activities if circumstances change due to a more engaging group that prefer more dialogue.

8. _____ I have a clear sense of how the training should proceed from start to finish, not only for each training seminar but also for the entire training program.

9. _____ I restructure training efforts where appropriate to ensure that the group is engaged and enjoying the training.

10. _____ I coordinated with participants and clients to assure steady progress on the training.

_____ TOTAL SCORE for Division of Work

Section 2: Authority

11. _____ I prepare complete module(s) that are about 45 minutes to one and half-hours for my training session(s).

12. _____ I try to anticipate what participants would apply in the future as a result of my training in leadership development.

13. _____ I establish clear goals for participants and myself.

14. _____ I carefully analyzed both the pros and cons of the decisions made to delivery this training.

15. _____ I am willing to be creative and innovative and try new things to expand my training platform.

16. ___ I had a clear vision for presenting my first opening introduction and accomplishing the training from beginning to end. With a story at the beginning and a strong closing.

17. ___ I put plans for modules on detailed power point slides with notes so that I have an exact placeholder for beginning the seminar, breaking points, and closure.

18. ___ I attempt to anticipate questions and obstacles to goal accomplishment such as having extra material and exercises in case there is extra time to fill toward the end of the seminar.

_____ TOTAL SCORE for Authority

Section 3: Discipline

19. _____ I discuss plans and involve clients, human resource directors, and managers in designing the seminar.

20. ___ I try to remain flexible by asking what is desired of the current topic that is spearheading the training at the beginning, so that I can adapt the training to concurrent conditions, and circle back at the end of the training session to ensure all points where covered.

21. ___ I provide a clear tracking of participants via attendance for those coming and going to ensure that all participants complete the training.

22. _____ At the end of each seminar, each participant receives a certificate with his or her name on it.

_____ TOTAL SCORE for Discipline

Section 4: Unity of command

23. ___ I set a protocol of questions and answers to be conducted throughout the seminar and keep track of progress and time to ensure that training is following a unified process.

_____ TOTAL SCORE for Unity of Command

Section 5: Unity of direction

24. ___ I set a professional demeanor as an example of excellent leadership for others to follow not only during the training but also after and before the training.

25. _____ I am effective at motivating others to not only complete the training, but also to stay engaged during the training, and apply the knowledge and competencies learned during the training.

26. _____ I try to keep a balance between giving participants individual attention and keeping a spirit of teamwork throughout the training.

27. ___ I handle conflict during the training seminar in a nonthreatening and constructive way by remaining calm, cool, and collected.

28. _____ I help the participants by providing them with guidance during the training to help them better perform their roles.

29. _____ I am a participative trainer, and I can adapt to the suggestions from participants, senior management, and clients.

30. _____ I keep senior management informed about the training activities and progress throughout the training.

31. _____ I showed a genuine interest in the work of all participants when conducting the seminars.

32. _____ I am considerate, engaging, motivational, and empathetic when providing constructive suggestions to seminar participants.

33. _____ I understand participant's needs and encourage their initiative in meeting those needs.

_____ TOTAL SCORE for Unity of Direction

Section 6: Subordination of individual interests to the general interest

34. ____ I attempt to transform participants to consider the greater good of their work and attempt to get them to sacrifice personal agendas for the overall organizational mission.

_____ TOTAL SCORE for Subordination of individual interests to the general interest

Section 7: Remuneration

35. ____ I set a professional training platform that does not consider pay or rank when discussion leadership development.

36. _____ I attempt to take note of promotions, recognition, or accolades that result in Return On Investment (ROI) when conducting training sessions without addressing pay scales.

_____ TOTAL SCORE for Remuneration

Section 8: Centralization

37.____ I encourage a cultural environment for the decision-making process that begins from the lower levels of the organization if possible.

38._____ When conducting training seminars, I attempt to treat all participants the same so that each one can have a voice.

_____ TOTAL SCORE for Centralization

Section 9: Scalar Chain

39.____ I set up a training platform that does not have to reach up the hierarchy for answers to leadership questions, but can reach across, reach down, and when appropriate, reach up to senior leadership.

_____ TOTAL SCORE for Scalar Chain

Section 10: Order

40. _____ I regularly assessed the return-on-investment (ROI) and progress on the training methods, exercises, and takeaways.

41. _____ I try to assure that the information that I use in training is timely, accurate, complete, and relevant to the organization and participants.

42. _____ I routinely share information with other trainers to ensure that we (as trainers) are using the state-of-the-art material.

43. _____ I compare progress with other trainers, and we learn from each other to take corrective action to improve training seminars as warranted.

44. _____ I managed my time when delivering a seminar and help participants manage their time to improve the seminar effectiveness.

45. _____ I have excellent sources of information or methods for obtaining information for training and use the most current and relevant information.

46. _____ I use technology (videos, power point slides, exercises, role-playing, surveys, case studies, etc.) to enhance the progress of the training and communicating well with participants.

47. _____ I anticipate the possibility of negative situations and scenarios to arise while training and I take immediate action to minimize them without being confrontational.

48. _____ I recognize that being proactive as opposed to reactive to prevent problems from occurring during training is a concern.

49. ____ I balance my training platform with both sequential steps and a global application to shape the training to fit participant-learning styles.

_____ TOTAL SCORE for Order

Section 11: Equity

50.___ I set up a training platform that does not encourage equitable concerns (i.e., pay status) by not talking about salary and rank while training yet I encourage participants to be engaged as a team with equal status.

_____ TOTAL SCORE for Equity

Section 12: Stability of tenure of personnel

51.___ I set up a strong emphasis of respect for authority figures among all the participants.

52.___ I emphasize the importance of personal staying power, being an advocate for the organization, and have a due diligence to always do the right thing.

_____ TOTAL SCORE for Stability of tenure of personnel

Section 13: Initiative

53.___ I encourage people to take initiative and apply what they learn during the training to enhance their career and return to the workplace with an action plan to use the new knowledge as soon as possible.

_____ TOTAL SCORE for Initiative

14. Esprit de corps

54.___ I set up a seminar that engages teamwork throughout the training by building camaraderie and extenuating a friendly working relationship with each other during training and encouraging this attitude afterward.

55.___ I initiate a sense of teamwork when working with clients, during seminars with participants, and after seminars as a follow-up mechanism to assess training performance.

_____ TOTAL SCORE for Esprit de corps

Self-Assessment Instrument Analysis - How Do I Rate as a Trainer?

This self-assessment has indicated your ability to train leaders effectively and efficiently. It will help you with your current understanding of your consulting practice of management and executive training competency. This assessment outlines fourteen key areas of training. The primary focus is on planning your seminar platform, organizing your training material, leading with your modules and sessions, and controlling your environment.

Now that you completed this task, calculate your total results for the each of the fourteen areas. Note your areas of strengths and weaknesses to help you develop your competency to be an expert leadership trainer.

After completing the analysis, review the following question to ensure that you are self-aware of your capability to train executives in leadership.

(1) What were your scores in each of the fourteen areas? How might you go about developing the competencies that indicated low score(s)?

SUMMARY:

If you scored a 150 or above, you are, either already a professional or you are ready for training. If you scored 125 or 149, take some time to plan and organize your training platform before venturing out. Below 125, read the rest of the book before considering training and management consulting. You may want to contact the author, Dr. Michael Provitera, to discuss your potential to train executives.

Your Highest Score

1: Division of work _ ____ 50
2: Authority 40
3: Discipline ____ 20
4: Unity of command 5
5: Unity of direction ____ 50
6: Subordination 5
7: Remuneration ____ 10

8: Centralization   10
9: Scalar Chain   5
10: Order   50
11: Equity   5
12: Stability   10
13: Initiative   5
14: Esprit de corps   10

Total Scores (You____; Highest 175)

Reference

[1] Pistrui, J., & Dimov, D. The Role of a Manager Has to Change in 5 Key Ways. *Harvard Business Review* (October, 2018).

[2] Kiechel, W. The Management Century. *Harvard Business Review* (November 2012)

[3] Birkinshaw, J., & Goddard, J. What Is Your Management Model? *MIT Sloan Management Review* (January, 2009).

[4] Mintzberg, H. The Manager's Job: Folklore and Fact. *Harvard Business Review* (March–April 1990).

[5] Haggerty, N., Wan, Z., & Wang Y. Cultivating Virtual Competence. *Ivey Business Review Journal* (November- December 2020).

[6] Glaveski, S. Where Companies Go Wrong with Learning and Development. *Harvard Business Review* (October, 2019).

[7] Bersin, J., & Zao-Sanders, M. Making Learning a Part of Everyday Work. *Harvard Business Review* (February, 2019).

[8] Kwok, N., & Shen, W. Leadership Training Shouldn't Just Be for Top Performers. *Harvard Business Review* (January, 2022).

[9] Singhel, T. The One Skill that Helped Me Grow in My Career. *Harvard Business Review* (February, 2019).

Chapter 2

Building a Foundation of Cultural Cohesiveness

Psychological contracts, originated by Chris Argris, in 1960, and further developed by Denise Rousseau in 1989 in the seminal paper "Psychological and implied contracts in organizations." Argris believed that employees and their organization created psychological contracts that allowed the expression and gratification of each other's needs.

The Psychological Contract changed between leaders and followers as a result of COVID-19. Remote work has risen as the most predominant concern along with keeping stakeholders safe during the pandemic. The post-pandemic recovery has created hybrid leadership models that incorporate both in-office and –remote communication. Electronic meetings have been also introduced as real-time think tanks that have exploited the Psychological Contract as the world recovers from the pandemic. The exploitation comes in the way of tacit correspondence between the leaders and followers. As a result, less is more, in this case. If you are doing well, less information needs to be communicated. Thus, leaving a void Psychological Contract that lingers on as the focus shifts to recovery and safety.

The importance of organizational resources is also escalated in the post-pandemic recovery. They have led to a new look at resilience as organizations recovery from COVID-19. The better the use of organizational resources to formulate a vision, and in some cases, a new mission statement, the more likely the post-pandemic recovery.

The State of Management Consulting

We asked management consultants what leaders do. Then, we ask leaders what management consultants do. The results, as you may expect, was not exact. Management Consultants viewed leaders as conceptualizing strategy with a personality type of A. They turned out to be across the gamut with human relationships and conceptualizing being almost equal. For the most part, they were type B personality. Leaders coined management consultants as modified executives with a global view of the organization. Turned out, management consultants were glorified trainers. They trained well, facilitated meetings better than other people internal to the organization, and they acted as change agents.

Scholars coined leaders as executives who engage in the facilitation of building and sustaining relationships with subordinates (Avolio, Waldman & Yammarino, 1991; Canty, 2005). There has been some connection with executive leadership and the management of knowledge. With Knowledge Management being a set of processes aimed at creating value through generating and applying intellectual capital (Marr, et al., 2003).

Management consultants focus on the mediating effects of organizational factors (i.e., culture, structure and strategy). Thus, we expose the relationship between organizational leadership and knowledge management.

The Post-Pandemic World

In a post pandemic world, culture is projected to include three dimensions. They are collaboration, trust, and learning (Neeley, 2021). By incorporating each of them together, an organization can recover from COVID-19. By enhancing collaboration and dialogue, and aligning the subordinate's individual interests with collective interests, people begin to build better relationships.

Technology led to people trusting systems that help executives lead better. Engender trust by focusing on identifying employee's individual needs. Leaders provide the freedom for employees to explore new ideas and knowledge (Horwitz, et al., 2008; Patiar & Mia, 2009). Thus, leadership, when done correctly, creates a continuous learning environment.

Collaboration is a necessary precursor to create new ideas and develop knowledge. This builds a trust-based organizational culture which is ideal for sharing tacit knowledge (Wenger, 1998). Leaders ability to create knowledge and develop a more innovative climate is important.

Consultants can share best practices and experiences (i.e., learning, technology, and presentation equipment) which is additional knowledge that inside trainers may not have. Thus, creating new knowledge for companies for the post

COVID-19 recovery. We found that organizations that emphasize the cultural aspect of learning are much stronger in generating new ideas and knowledge.

As mentioned, in the previous chapter, decentralized structures preceded the pandemic, but we found it became more prevalent in the post-pandemic as organizations are attempting to reset the office structure. As noted, leaders achieve a higher degree of effectiveness in a decentralized structure. Thus, executives that develop decentralized structures with the aim of improving knowledge sharing and creating a more innovative climate have been able to recover quickly and effectively. Through training and development, leaders inspire and transform aggregate human capital into social capital in order to implement the required changes that are necessary for continuous improvement. As mentioned in the previous chapter, highly centralized structures are more bureaucratic, and this, negatively contributes to the effectiveness of leadership when a turbulent environment exists.

When an organization has an open climate, employees ae able to exchange new ideas. During COVID-19, this was done via email communication, instant messenger, and text. Pre-meeting and post meeting communicated was enhanced with this technology. This has impacted the way people view webinars, online training, and even simulation-type exercises, because once the information and clarification are disseminated, then the employees immediately implement ideas through the delegation of authority to their departments to the lowest levels possible and improve successful execution (Cardinal, 2001; Sivadas & Dwyer, 2000).

Many consultants base their practice on tenets that they deem successful. Our experience, working with executives, surfaces four pillars of strategy that we feel are important. They are analysis, defensiveness, futurity, and pro-activeness. Analysis strategy attempts to meet the goals of intellectual stimulation, a focal point of transformational leadership, which seeks to provide new and innovative solutions for organizational problems. As organizations emphasized resilience which we found moving in tandem with operational risk management.

During the pandemic, financial risk management illuminated but the operational risk superseded as organizations struggled for survival. Thus, leaders developed a futurity strategy as a more comprehensive vision of the future. Some mission and vision statements were altered for con-current pandemic concerns.

Leaders also apply a defensive strategy to implement the required modifications in order to efficiently use organizational resources, decrease costs and control the resources. Pro-activeness and futurity strategies inspire employees to investigate better solutions and opportunities not only during a crisis, but also during non-turbulent times. Leaders set high expectations, providing a suitable situation for followers to identify new opportunities.

Analysis strategy plays a critical role in accumulating organizational knowledge, including both processes of knowledge creation and acquisition. Knowledge management requires a continuous investigation of a SWOT analysis. Strengths, weaknesses, opportunities, and threats provide an indication that knowledge can be enhanced, quantified, and stored effectively so that it can be useful when it is needed.

For example, a defensiveness approach enhances efficiency through reusing knowledge to reduce organizational costs (Zheng, Yang & Mclean, 2010). One defensiveness approach was in helping many people select early retirement through incentives.

Thus, when consulting, a futurity strategy could promote the process of knowledge application by providing a series of guidelines for companies, aiming at tracking trends, conducting "what-if" analysis, allocating capabilities and adapting actions. Then, having the participants follow-up at their business units for implementation of ideas for improvement. When conducing executive leadership training, a model can serve the process better than a power point slide with bells and whistles.

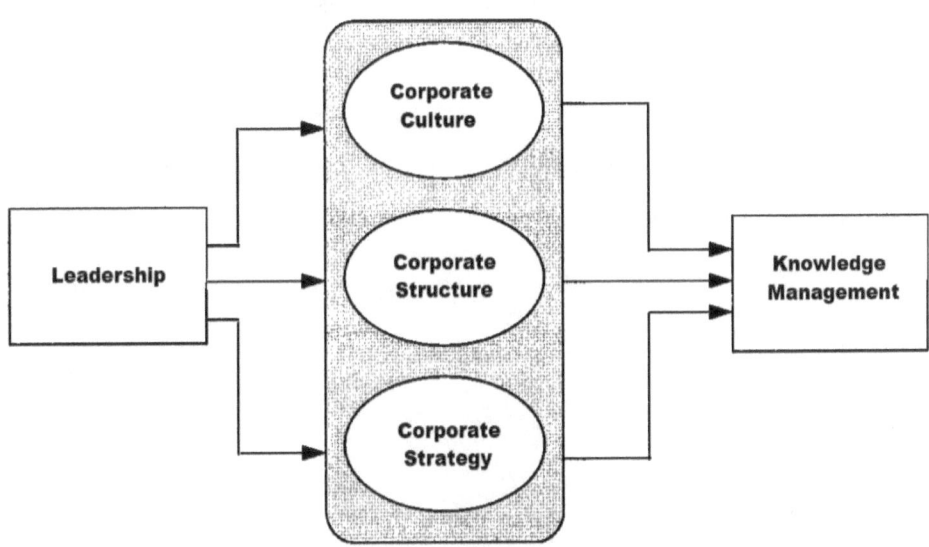

CONCLUSION

This chapter begins with the managerial consultant establishing a psychological contract with the client. Highlighting the vital importance of leadership to stimulate a cohesive culture of learning and development as many followers are working remotely, builds upon collaboration, providing trust for remote workers as they wonder what the future looks like. The model above is one way to build the managerial consulting practice that is both effective and timely.

The flattened workforce is extended to the home office, and this has an impact on the need to improve strategies within organizations.

Chapter 3

Expanding the Management Consultant's Black Box

Leadership development has led to a salivating audience with a wondering group of management consultants rebranding, augmenting services, and adding flexible delivery platforms. A long time ago, a prominent scholar responded, by the name of J. Barney, in 1991, a presidential professor of strategic management at The University of Utah, presented executives with a slew of internal resources that provided a direct vision for the organization. Barney published his work on *Firm Resources and Sustained Competitive Advantage* in the renowned Journal of Management. Thus, from prior research, we know that a sustainable competitive advantage is always warranted by executives. Yet a complication comes about because competitive advantage is stymied when things become more turbulent. This complication is of concern because as many executives sit at home running billion-dollar businesses so do their followers, customers, suppliers, and all the other stakeholders. The prior research, therefore, failed to provide a comprehensive framework which incorporates all the internal resources that may simultaneously impact leadership development, especially during a pandemic.

There is a gap in the business literature in examining the implications of structure, culture, strategy, inter-corporate social networks and stakeholder orientation for leadership development.

The course of action to address this concern entails evidence from our research that suggests that the following organizational characteristics will contribute to the literature on a firms competitive advantage by including organizational structure, organizational culture, strategic management, Inter-organizational social networks, and stakeholder orientation. A recent Harvard Business Review study found that relational and communication skills are much in need today and we address this concern by adding color on social networking within organizations.

> **The need for leadership development has never been more urgent. Companies of all sorts realize that to survive in today's volatile, uncertain, complex, and ambiguous environment, they need leadership skills and organizational capabilities different from those that helped them succeed in the past. There is also a growing recognition that leadership development should not be restricted to the few who are in or close to the C-suite. With the proliferation of collaborative problem-solving platforms and digital "adhocracies" that emphasize individual initiative, employees across the board are increasingly expected to make consequential decisions that align with corporate strategy and culture. It's important, therefore, that they be equipped with the relevant technical, relational, and communication skills.** (Moldoveanu and Narayandas, 2021)

Understanding the implications of equipping leaders with the most relevant technical skills coupled with relational and communication skills provide a significant contribution to the business literature, especially in developing a new and dynamic conception of a company's characteristics within the leadership development paradigm. Thus, building a management consultants black box and extending the knowledge to their clients.

Expanding the management consultant's black box could consist of a plethora of iterations. We propose the five that we use, which are corporate structure, corporate culture, corporate strategy, inter-corporate social networks, and corporate strategy.

First **Corporate Structure.** Leaders inspire followers to generate new solutions and a more cohesive environment (Eagly & Carli, 2003). As mentioned earlier, a highly centralized structure has a negative impact on leadership, while decentralization positively contributes to leaders in developing a more innovative climate. Decentralized structures facilitate the exchange of ideas and the implementation of more innovative solutions based on stipulating the power of decision-making at all levels of the organization. This is the platform in which great management consultants are built upon.

However, a management consultant should not turn down a client with a tall structure. Management consultants can have a long history of client needs as they attempt to build more teamwork and organic structures. These types of organizations can have a highly formalized structures, they are more bureaucratic, and this negatively contributes to the development of leadership in changing the existing situations and creating a better environment (Jung et al., 2008).

Thus, management consultants are more effective in

more informal structures when compared to bureaucratic structures. Hence, while a management consultant may be in need at a formalized and centralized structure, the structure itself is negatively related to the development of leadership.

Second, **Corporate Culture,** in which we primarily focus upon how trust is an important component of a collaborative culture. Trust positively contributes to developing and maintaining organizational communication. As followers trust their leaders, they become more familiar and loyal to policy and procedures, speak up more often, and feel more informed when dealing with both daily and future job requirements.

Thus, both cultural aspects, collaboration, and trust can be critical for leadership development, which is strongly based on developing relationships with subordinates (Canty, 2005). An organization's shared beliefs and values that have been established by the leaders of the organization can be reinforced through training and development. Training and development can be reinforced through various methods of delivery (i.e., break-out sessions, group dialogue, and open discussions, and presentation dialogue addressing a concern), ultimately shaping employee perceptions, behaviors, and understanding.

Moreover, leader's ability to build a more innovative environment is also highly dependent on the extent to which their subordinates trust them. Corporate culture that instills trust in subordinates enables leaders to mobilize their follower's support toward the leadership vision for changing or enhancing current situations, whereas distrust will impair leadership development (Bass & Avolio, 1997; Bennis & Nanus, 1985). Therefore, both cultural aspects of collaboration and trust can positively contribute to leadership.

Corporate Strategy is a topic that we sometimes have a strong impact upon, especially at the beginning of a fiscal year. It depends on whether senior leadership is involved or not in the training platform. In most cases, the Human Resource director is our main communication. On occasion, we also have influence, or direct contact, with upper echelon leadership. One area that we focused our attention on when training leaders is identifying four aspects that we found to be illuminating, especially during COVID19. The four factors are *Analysis, Pro-activeness, Defensiveness, and Futurity*.

The way we train using the *Analysis* factor, we aim to find the best solution for solving strategic problems or implementing strategic objectives using the problematic search of various options (Zheng, Yang & McLean 2010). This is done as a group with a vision board and strengths, weaknesses, opportunities, and threats (SWOT Analysis) identified by groups. Once the analysis is complete, we discuss opportunities and how to implement them. We found that leadership vision and mission is affected by the problematic search of various alternatives and patterns to solve organizational problems. This method became effective as our clients addressed the post-pandemic recovery (Sayyadi

& Provitera, 2021b).

Futurity strategy is used as a method of applying the opportunities, which can also augment threats and weaknesses, and expand on strengths. In effect, we focus on the leader's ability to develop a more future-oriented vision for their organization (Venkatraman, 1989). Analysis and futurity may have a positive impact on leadership development.

Participants find that analysis strategy creates more knowledge, and this can improve leadership effectiveness through generating more innovative solutions for both organizational problems and strategic development (Zheng, 2005).

When COVID19 first arrived, executives mentioned that leadership effectiveness can be improved through taking a proactive approach that searches for better strategic initiatives.

An addition to our training during the COVID19 pandemic is ***Inter-Corporate Social Networks***. We found that when we had large groups of employees from different business units that the collaboration among them increase tremendously. Executive expressed that inter-corporate social networking improved their leadership effectiveness in developing a more innovative climate, primarily, because of the sharing of ideas. During trainings, like offsite meetings, participants felt that inter-corporate social networks had a positive impact on leader's viewpoints and motivated them to expand relationships with their subordinates. Thus, Inter-corporate social networks enable leaders to establish a more cohesive relationships with subordinates, providing a wider array of empowerment for their followers. This is not new, however, departments linked together by using inter-corporate social networks providing an awareness of becoming more capable in the effectiveness of learning leadership concepts has been around since Frederick Taylor created coined the phrase "the one best way" in his work in the area of scientific management (Purvis, Sambamurthy & Zmud 2000).

When management consultants consider a **Stakeholder Orientation**, they are certainly addressing a larger group of people, but any consultant worth his or her weight needs to consider all possible people involved. Taking a stakeholder orientation provides a thorough understanding of the departments, the clients need, the customer, and all constituents. The way we use stakeholder orientation is an important aspect of leadership development, especially during post-Covid-19. We attempt to give everyone a voice in decision making so that we can increase buy-in.

Stakeholder orientation, can improve leadership development through developing a better vision that incorporates stakeholder's attitudes, facilitates knowledge sharing, and provides for both creativity and innovation. The innovation component of executive training is dependent on exchanging as much knowledge and obtaining as much feedback as possible, from various stakeholders. Exchanging knowledge can have a strong influence on learning within organizations (Purvis, Sambamurthy & Zmud 2000). We found that many executives talked often with their competitors, and many of them are friends, sharing best practices. In fact, the best trainings are those that have an array of executives working together from different organizations attempting to solve world problems. The reason for this scenario is because the amount of knowledge exchanged with various stakeholders may be more likely to contribute to the development of leadership in identifying better opportunities in the current and future business environment.

CONCLUSION

Expanding the management consultant's black box is a huge part of this book. This chapter exemplified four tools that can be placed directly in the box. Building the raptor of consulting can be found in the book titled Level-UP Leadership: Trainer's Manual, authored by Dr. Michael Provitera. This chapter, while it is all encompassing of a leadership development training, captures the development of leaders as they attempt to sustain the negative impact of the Covid-19 pandemic.

The five elaborative insights for management consultants offered by modeling how leadership development can enhance organizational characteristics, is captured in the four tenets----corporate structure, corporate culture, corporate strategy covered in the previous chapter, and this chapter introduces Inter-corporate social networks. Whether you are beginning your practice, or you are a seasoned management consultant, incorporating these four tenets will enhance your practice.

Chapter 4

Becoming a Transformational Leadership Consultant

When training leaders, one of our main go-to is transformational leadership. There is something about that model that grabs the attention of executives. We often train on two models and then ask participants which one they like best and about 75 to 90 percent stick with transformational leadership.

It is important to touch upon the foundation of leadership before delving into models of leadership. The true basis of leadership was built upon a model that generated two sides of an X and Y axis. On one side is the concept of leadership that creates change through taking a process-oriented viewpoint and the other as more of a relationship-oriented approach.

It is also imperative to briefly touch upon the negative side of leadership, which in some cases, may be transformational leadership, according to some scholars. However, the black hat of leadership, synonymous with the negative effect that a charismatic leader has on followers. Adolf Hitler, Fidel Castro, and Vladimir Putin, to mention a few.

While transactional leadership involves determining the tasks, rewarding goal achievement, and punishing failure in attaining goals (Eagly & Carli, 2003), transformational leadership focuses on the critical human assets such as commitment and thus helps followers to effectively implement organizational change with both efficiency and effectiveness (Yukl, and Van Fleet, 1992).

Another aspect of leadership worth noting while

training is autocratic and democratic styles of leadership. Just like both transactional and transformational, autocratic and democratic style of leadership may be necessary at times.

Our focus, however, is on transformational leadership. The first thing we do is introduce the definition by Yukl and Van Fleet (1992, p. 174):

> "Transformational leadership is the process of influencing major changes in the attitudes and assumptions of organization members (organization culture) and building commitment for major changes in the organization's objectives and strategies".

Transformational leaders have been known to turn a weak business plan into a success, but a poor leader can ruin even the best plan. During some trainings, we use case studies, depending on the participants. One example of this comes from CEO Rich Teerlink, who dramatically transformed Harley-Davidson, and fundamentally built a different organization that still prospers today. The success of leadership at the Harley-Davidson Corporation has stood the test of time. For example, Harley-Davidson's leadership created a more effective organization built upon three primary principles: 1) focusing on people, 2) challenging norms, and 3) continuing to fundamentally change. At Harley, every employee can participate in leadership decision-making.

Another example, we use, of a transformational leader in a highly competitive environment is Steve Jobs, former

CEO of the Apple, who built a highly effective organization through taking a change-oriented leadership approach, which highly manifested itself in building a talented staff, new product development, cohesive organizational structure, and intense marketing.

Evidence from these examples resonate with participants suggesting that transformational leadership is highly demanded at the corporate level. Participants also feel that enlightened and empowered leadership gives them a chance for innovativeness and creativity. This concept can also be manifested in knowledge integration. Van de Ven (2017), argues that "Knowledge integration, which is the purposeful combination of specialized and complementary knowledge to achieve specific tasks, is becoming increasingly important for organizations facing rapidly changing institutional environments, globalized markets, and fast-paced technological developments." In a recent webinar, on March 12, 2022, Van de Ven expressed how he encountered many CEOs, but one resonated with him that he felt inclined to mention. Andrew talked about Lewis Lehr, a Chairman and CEO of 3M company. He called Lehr a truly enlightened CEO, in the early 1980s. He felt that Lehr was a person that was like a knight of the CEOs at that time.

> "Lewis Lehr, CEO, was very open, very inquisitive, and very willing to challenge his top managers and district directors to start new businesses and engage in others.

An enlightened and empowered CEO makes a huge difference in an organization." (Direct quote from Andrew Van de Ven)

CEOs, like Bill Gates, managed intellectual capital. He once was noted for saying that if he lost his top 50 people that he would not have an organization anymore.

Transformational leaders identify employee's needs and show concern for both organizational needs and follower's interests concurrently. When transformational leaders show concern for the employee's individual needs, individuals begin to contribute more commitment and they become more inspired, and they put extra effort into their work. This extra effort improves the quality of products, customer satisfaction, and impacts shareholder value and improves operational risk management.

Transformational leaders use intellectual capital and social capital to develop extraordinary organizational communication aimed at providing valuable resources for stakeholders. Knowledge sharing of intellectual capital, once identified, is shared. Sharing best practices that are positive in nature and sharing negative practices that are coined to be avoided going forward, has an extraordinary impact on both performance and innovation. Negative outcomes are to be tolerated to some extent if innovation and creativity is going to be fostered at any organization. Empowered and enlightened employees respond to environmental changes, which in turn, enhances firm performance regarding return on assets and return on equity.

Transformational Leadership Consulting

The future of transformational leadership training is increasing. To grasp the knowledge of executives worldwide, the Association of Executive Search Consultants (AESC), in 2020, surveyed business leaders to identify the current and new challenges faced now in 2023, and up to 2025. The results highlighted the significant role of leadership for organizations and confirmed that business leaders identified leadership effectiveness as one of the main areas for using an outside consultant. This opens opportunity for outside vendors soliciting consulting gigs and creates a need in the human resource department to develop talent within to meet the need for leadership training.

Martin Schubert (cited in AESC, 2020, p. 5), a partner at Eric Salmon & Partners, states that:

> "In technology, in industry, in financial services, even in consumer goods and life sciences, experiencing a change in their business models that are much more global, much more virtual, with diminishing hierarchies that require a different leadership type. And this drives both leadership advisory and executive search."

Considering the increased pressures of the global workplace that inspires leaders to drive effective change at the organizational level, opportunities for transformational leadership consulting grow as organizations are increasingly participating in international markets. For example, Dorota Czarnota (cited in AESC, 2020), a Country Manager at Russell Reynolds Associates sees high potential for growing transformational leadership consulting in Latin America, Europe, Asia, and Africa.

Management consultants can manifest a broad spectrum of leadership development techniques. Transformational leadership has been highlighted as the behavior indicative of friendship, mutual trust, respect, and warmth. Building a consulting practice on this foundation will lead to a wide array of opportunity. Thus, the key to transformational leadership is based upon satisfying basic needs and verbalizing feelings of admiration, respect and trust toward themselves to meet higher desires through inspiring followers to provide newer solutions and create a better workplace.

Transformational leadership took off in 1978 with Burns (1978), when he initially developed the concept of transformational leadership. More recently, transformational leadership has been developed by scholars, such as Eagly and Carli (2003), Avolio and Luthans (2021), and Patiar and Mia (2009), and we feel that this field is continuing to evolve.

Charismatic leadership can be taught. Although,

charismatic leadership is a sister of transformational leadership, it has many critics identifying the bad apples that placed the wrong connotation on leadership using charisma. The key is to train Transformational leaders to influence employee's individual interests to align their goals and objectives with institutional interests, and through inspiring followers to create new ideas and innovations for effective business outcomes.

Whether charismatic, transformational, or both, treating human capital as individuals builds role models that are trusted, admired, and respected by followers. These role models become organizational advocates.

Training Executives in Transformational Leadership

There are many ways to incorporate transformational leadership into your training. We showcase the four techniques of transformational leadership as the forefront and knowledge base. Through these four techniques, participants grasp the foundational knowledge and then attempt to apply what they learn to the workplace. These four techniques include:

1. Idealized influence, the goal here is to influence behavior,
2. Individualized consideration, specifying specific skills that are unique to the individual and celebrating them,

3. Intellectual stimulation, taking people to levels of leadership that they have not been but may want to explore, and;
4. Inspirational motivation, ensuring success for everyone at all stages of their career.

When building the ***idealized influence*** platform, aim to develop a shared vision and improve relationships with followers. In doing this technique, executives need to take the following actions:

- Instill pride in organizational members for being associated with them.
- Display a sense of power and confidence in everyone.
- Go beyond self-interest for the good of the organization.
- Talk about and address their most important values and beliefs.
- Consider the moral and ethical consequences of decision making.
- Emphasize the importance of having a collective sense of mission.
- improve knowledge management initiatives and keep employees satisfied, equitable, and engaged.

When building the ***individualized consideration,*** concentrate on identifying employee's individual needs and empowering followers in order to build a learning organization and mobilizing follower support and trust toward the goals and objectives. In doing this technique, executives need to take the following actions:

- Spend time coaching others.
- Consider employees as having different needs, abilities, and aspirations.
- Help organizational members to develop their strengths, manage opportunities, avoid threats, and provide various formal training programs to improve their performance.

Management consultants also need to make deliberate attempts to inspire executives to use ***intellectual stimulation*** through developing effective mechanisms to propel knowledge sharing in the organization and generate more innovative ideas and solutions for new and demanding issues that come up constantly in our hypercompetitive economic environment. In doing this technique, executives need to take the following actions:

- Place an emphasis on the effective coordination among different functional areas and seek differing

perspectives when solving problems.
- Suggest new ways of looking at how to complete assignments and undertake a comprehensive analysis when confronting important decisions.
- Find novel ways to create reading of pertinent information and help people develop the skills of research when seeking answers to organizational problems.

The fourth key for management consultants is building the ***inspirational motivation*** platform and focus on inspiring people and not just treating them as human assets with a social security number. Obtain suggestions for improvement and integrate suggestions into the decisions regarding how to set a higher level of desired expectations. In doing this technique, executives need to take the following actions:

- Talk optimistically about the future.
- Talk enthusiastically about what needs to be accomplished.
- Express confidence that the goals will be achieved.
- Address current situations at the organization, around the world, and how these things may influence organizational success, and they draw attention away from the negative things that pry on people's minds and move them to be more productive.

These four techniques of transformational leadership, when carried out correctly from the training podium, can present a set of practice for an effective leadership development.

The key is to develop people to be effective leaders that work in today's knowledge-based economy that is dynamic and constantly changing. This training platform will develop intellectual capital in organizations.

CONCLUSION

Becoming a management consulting and expanding your practice to utilize transformational leadership training is more of an art than a science. Scholars and practitioners embrace transformational leadership training as it meets the needs of many facets of leadership development.

When considering leadership development as a process, the trainer takes the focus off the bottom line, the revenue, and places it in the hands of the participants to learn, grow, develop, and soar in their careers.

Focusing just on revenue leaves participants with a one-sided approach to leadership. The tenets of transformational leadership are vast and boundaryless.

Chapter 5

Becoming an Authentic Leadership Development Consultant

Authentic leadership has picked up steam over the past decades as leaders want to see a frank appellation of their leadership prowess. This is nothing new because leadership has always been at the forefront management training (Mills, 2005). While leadership stands out above management, actually, the four functions of management depict leadership as one of the four. For instance, Henri Fayol has been posited as the forefather of the functions of management. While he had more than four in his original publication in France which was translated to English in the 1930s. The four that seemed to stand the test of time are controlling, leading, planning, and organizing.

Leadership, being a strong component of management has manifested in the forefront of many executives and aspiring leaders. There are more reasons than one that Fayol included leadership as a function of management. For example, in Steven Markham's (2012) view, leadership stems from ancient history. The concept of leadership highly manifested itself in ancient extended families that constructed clans as the central ingredient of cities such as Rome, Italy. The role of leadership was considerably centralized, and membership in the clans was highly demanding in order to be successful in the social institutions.

Many scholars and practitioners ask the question "Can leaders be made, or do they have to be born leaders to be successful?" Before attempting to answer this question, let us agree that leaders can be made and that being a born leader may be an additional attribute of leadership. Now, answering the question. Leaders are born and so are professors, trainers, doctors, and all other professions. To say leaders, have to be born leaders in order to be successful is an oversight.

While Fayol captured the essence of leadership in his functions of management, leadership is not a new phenomenon. Warren Bennis (2009) illustrates, in an attempt to differentiate the concepts of leadership and management. He argued that while a leader acquires his competencies by embracing education, a manager becomes familiar with managerial activities by undergoing training. He asserts that the education system is more strategic, synthetic, experimental, flexible, active, and broad when compared to training principles that manifest themselves in being passive, narrow, and rote. Bennis's notion is an interesting perspective because an organization will train managers their own way, but there are some exceptions in which organizations incorporate education in training. We certainly do, at **Motivational Leadership Training**, but with caution because we attempt to facilitate more than teach.

Some scholars feel that there is a profound difference between leaders and managers. A leader, in fact, takes a proactive approach towards more strategic goals, and evokes expectations of followers to follow in the direction of being influenced and coached by them.

Leadership focuses on challenging the current norms

and motivating employees. Followers, therefore, are trained in leadership as intellectual capital to think about organizational issues in a more innovative and creative manner.

Followers need to develop a trust-based relationship to be willing to share their knowledge and new ideas with others.

Management and leadership are not different. Henry Mintzberg (2007), an author and scholar in the area of management at McGill University, in Canada, feels that they are not so different and being a manager is being a leader.

Joseph Rost (1991) conceptualizes management as an authority relationship between at least one manager and one subordinate who coordinates their activities to produce and to sell particular goods or provide some type of service. Management emphasizes more operational objectives rather than simply investigating strategic goals. Therefore, management has been highlighted as an authority relationship to maintain the status quo through coordinating and controlling subordinate activities. There is much more to management and most titles stipulate the word management, not leadership.

This is where some scholars part ways. Once the status quo is mentioned, it appears that management is stagnant and overly consuming in nature. It is not, we agree with Mintzberg who once mentioned at the Academy of Management that differentiating leadership from management may be a way to repackage a program or degree and not an actual difference worthy of breaking away from management.

Management and leadership are one in the same and to be a good manager a person has to also be a good leader.

It is important for trainers to be aware of the current definitions on the concept of leadership and management, especially, given the fact that they are both posed as somewhat different by scholars.

Leadership, from the most basic definition as "influencing interactions with groups of followers to implement changes and achieve determined goals and objectives," to its most broad definition of "***influencing behavior***," has its roots in every aspect of our daily lives. Scholars are experts in management and leadership but very few take pride in being scholars of both, except for Henry Fayol, who would fall into the category of a management historian. Henry blended both theory and practice when management consulting and, perhaps, the modern management consultant practices with some theory and how that theory applies to practice.

The most controversial leadership model that depicts management and leadership is a model that generated two sides of an X and Y axis. On one side is the concept of leadership that creates change through taking a process-oriented and the other as more of a relationship-oriented approach. Scholars built the foundation of leadership based upon these two axes.

When trainers decide to draw upon the knowledge of authentic leadership and determine their competencies aimed at answering the question of how management consultants can play a strategic role in developing authentic leadership within companies, we encourage them to peruse the book "True North," which is a viable option. "**Discover Your True North**" is the best-selling leadership classic, by Bill George, that enables people to become an authentic leader by discovering their *True North*. Take a look:

> *Being a leader is about much more than a title and having management skills—it's fundamentally a question of who we are as human beings. The book, Discover Your True North, offers a concrete and comprehensive program for becoming an authentic leader and shows how to chart your path to leadership success.___Bill George*

Training Platforms with Authentic Leadership

As mentioned above, the prominent scholar on authentic leadership is Bill George (2003) who sheds light on authentic leaders as those chief executive officers who truly perceive their own values and beliefs and are highly recognized by other people as being aware of their own and their follower's values, strengths, and weaknesses. Authentic leaders are most knowledgeable about themselves and the context in which they lead. This leadership style takes place at the organizational level, and it can be shared at all levels (Hmieleski, Cole, & Baron, 2012).

When training participants on authentic leadership, draw from these tenets to build a strong foundation:

- Positive psychological capital
- Life Stories
- Positive moral perspective
- Self-awareness
- Leadership process
- Behavioral management
- Self-regulation
- Follower development, and
- Organizational context.

In this platform, management consultants develop a positive work climate in which followers more effectively contribute to a firm's performance and competitive advantage. Focus on authentic decision-making processes, which identifies moral dilemmas, and then evaluates and selects the best available alternative to be implemented.

Help participants continually understand their own beliefs, strengths, desires, values, and aspirations. This builds upon the authentic leadership framework and begins to open up engaging dialogue.

Authentic leaders can effectively influence their followers through positive social exchange. Taking note of emotional intelligence, by Dan Goleman, management consultants should at least be aware of self-awareness and self-regulation by which authentic leaders effectively align their core values and individual interests with institutional interests. Being transparent between leaders and followers is at the core of authentic leadership---even during tumultuous times Thus, authentic leader takes on a coaching role for transforming and developing people. Authentic leaders attempt to develop effective workplaces that promote the depth and range of knowledge access and sharing best practices, tools, and techniques, by providing equal opportunity for followers. Authentic leadership is also at the heart of diversity, equity, and inclusion training. Being authentic brings out the unabashed self.

CONCLUSION

This chapter raises vital questions as to how executives can effectively lead companies in today's hypercompetitive business environment. For management consultants, this chapter can portray a more detailed picture of the authentic leadership model and how it can be used for diversity, equity, and inclusiveness training.

Building upon self-awareness and understanding one's strengths and weaknesses can have a profound effect on not only the leader's career success but also his or her follower's career success.

Finding your own true north as a trainer is tantamount

to your success. Train what you love and love what you train or someone else will be training it without you.

Chapter 6

Serving Clients as a Management Consultant

Servant Leadership, a sister of Authentic Leadership, resonates well in the C-Suite as executives turn the organizational chart upside down. This is nothing new, but it became more apparent with the United States of America turning to diversity, inclusion, and equity, after the George Floyd incident that led to massive protests.

> May 25, 2020 — Minneapolis police officers respond to a call shortly after 8 p.m. about a possible counterfeit $20 bill being used at a corner grocery and encounter a Black man, later identified as George Floyd, who struggles and ends up handcuffed and face down on the ground. Officer Derek Chauvin presses his knee into Floyd's neck for about nine minutes while bystanders shout at him to stop. Video shows Floyd crying "I can't breathe" multiple times before going limp. He's pronounced dead at a hospital.

Many people do not know the specifics of this event, but one mention of the name George Floyd, and everyone knows it is related to police brutality at its worst.

Addressing this incident is not necessary as a trainer but being aware of it is a prerequisite today. Besides the local appeal to diversity awareness, equity, and inclusion, there is also a massive the global appeal to making work and communities safer and less confrontational. Therefore, as a trainer, develop a training platform with the Servant Leadership model and consider the global appeal and vision for all organizations to be mindful of mankind. [1]

Servant leadership expands micro-leadership models and espouses the broader global context that adheres to serving people of lesser means. This model has been developed to turn the organizational chart upside down, placing the CEO at the bottom of the chart, serving each unit, leading to the top of the chart, the customer.

Trainers need to develop the leadership mindset that helps leaders to begin to think globally, yet act locally, in an attempt to meet the needs of the local community and as they align with the global economic integration. Servant leadership plays a critical role and is a strategic prerequisite for business success in global markets as cultural differences determine the necessary business processes to meet the needs of the customer.

Management consultants use training as a tool to address the broad conversation of diversity, equity, and inclusion, and training is another way to do just that. Attempting to break down the silos amongst many organizations, going beyond managing the status quo, which limits the potential to adapt to today's uncertain business environment. [2] Servant leadership, thus, attempts to address the global need to investigate leadership styles and models to accomplish sustainable competitiveness in global markets.

Training executives is somewhat challenging because they already have a strong grasp on leadership. Engaging them in an attempt to help them become more effective is the objective and servant leadership is one leadership model in which the leader serves not only the customer but also the people that report to them.

Management consultants attempting to build a platform that incorporates some aspects of servant leadership will familiarize themselves with Robert Greenleaf. Greenleaf, first wrote an essay that later became his book titled *"Servant Leadership: a Journey into the Nature of Legitimate Power and Greatness."* [3] He introduced the term 'servant leadership' into the business literature for the first time and this caused some controversy in the corporate boardroom while adding some value among the leadership of the religious clergy.

Greenleaf was not only a scholar introducing this concept, but servant leadership also came out of his work experiences at organizations such as MIT and the influence of Hermann Hesse's *Journey to the East*. [4] Greenleaf largely gained his insights through the central character of 'Leo,' who becomes a servant leader and speaks about the Law of Service. The book notes as Leo characterizes:

He who wishes to live long must serve, but he who wishes to rule does not live long.

Greenleaf recognized the main message of this story and concluded that "The central meaning of it was that a great leader has experience as a servant to others, and he felt that this fact is central to his or her greatness. True leadership emerges from those whose primary motivation is a deep desire to help others." [3]

Thus, in a world filled with a strong attention to diversity, inclusion, and equity, servant leaders attempt to turn the organizational chart upside down, placing the customers at the top and helping the least among us---the employees, clients, and customers from lower means and social status. However, this logic has some employees feeling disjointed and unrecognized which opens up another avenue, beyond leadership development, to address anti-racism, diversity, and equity training platforms. An example of this logic comes from a company with over 2.3 million employees, Walmart. The famous Walmart mantra is be prepared for your bosses to arrive the store opens, giving employees a sense of meaninglessness and placing customers as additional bosses. [5]

When training using the Servant Leadership model, consider showcasing Greenleaf, who argues that the great leader is seen as a servant first, and that simple fact is the key to his or her greatness. The advantages of the servant leadership model are its altruism, simplicity, and self-awareness. It emphasizes the moral sense of concern for others, reducing the complexity engendered by putting personal desires in conflict with those of followers. Servant leadership can be clearly seen as rooted in the clergical leadership perspective in that of Christ's leadership. Thus, when Greenleaf says that the words "service," "to serve" and "servant" occur over 1300 times in the revised version of the St. James bible.

Use trepidation when deciding on training with the following statements, however, but you must understand it as a management consultant because some people in the training room may want a higher spiritual-like training as opposed to others. Knowing about spirituality in the workplace, not training on that subject, is important so that if challenged when training, you are knowledgeable about the origin. One time, Ken Blanchard, the world-renowned management trainer, ended his seminar with "God Bless" and turned off some people in the training session. This was after a great training platform up to that point in time. For example, Jesus once said:

> "Whoever wants to become great among you must be your servant, and whoever wants to be first must be your slave---just as the Son of Man did not come to be served, but to serve and to place his life as a ransom for many."

This is deep training and should only be positioned for those clients that area aware of universal applications of spirituality. However, knowing this as a consultant is key but practicing it is just as important as delivering the material in a training platform. The key is to touch on the servant leadership model, if you and your client feel comfortable, highlight Jesus as an ultimate example of a servant leader, and suggest applying the leadership insights that Jesus gives us within organizations. [6] [7] On the other hand, it may be better to reserve this lecture for a more clergical group such as a church or religious association.

According to the servant leadership model, only service to others, is the pathway to real significance. Management consultants need to first know that Michele Lawrence and Larry Spears in their book, *Practicing Servant Leadership: Succeeding Through Trust, Bravery, and Forgiveness*, concentrate on the characteristics of a servant leader, and recommend ten fundamental characteristics [8]:

1. Listening with the whole person in mind
2. Empathy for all people and especially the least among us
3. Healing with words, actions, and insight
4. Awareness of not only current events, but also of past events that are the focus of today's diversity, inclusion, and equity
5. Persuasion on the part of the person becoming better at everything they do, especially helping others
6. Conceptualization of the fact that we need to serve others, and this is more important than the golden rule or the platinum rule

7. Foresight into what the person needs at the moment, in the future, and discernment for what matters most for that individual and the good of society at large
8. Stewardship as a method of gathering people with like mindedness and attempting to bring others to the table
9. Commitment to the growth of not only oneself, but growth of all people, and;
10. Building community so that the thought helping others to be successful is passed on to generations.

Greenleaf, as mentioned early, the founder of servant leadership, acknowledges some criticisms about servant leadership, and posits that:

> "In a time of crisis, like the leadership crisis we are now in today, if too many potential builders are taken in by a complete absorption with dissecting the wrong and by a zeal for instant perfection, then the movement so many of us want to see will be set back. The danger, perhaps, is to hear the analyst too much and artist too little." [3]

Thus, we need to be creative when attempting to right the wrongs of society. We need to act out in artistry to help us deal with the past, make the present more livable, and the future, more prosperous for all walks of life.

The Servant leadership model has not evaded the criticism by scholars that normally are associated with leadership models and theories. [9] [10]

This model has been challenged for a lack of adequate empirical studies to substantiate its academic rigor and is often shelved as a learning tool as opposed to other leadership applications when management consulting contracts are drawn.

An example of this scholarly debate indicates that servant leadership is systematically undefined and lacking in empirical support necessary for managerial implementation. The existing literature on servant leadership is filled with anecdotal evidence and empirical research is critically needed to substantiate the use of it in the boardroom of large corporations. Therefore, if used in leadership development training, use it with caution and make note of its limitations.

Two main criticisms are important as the world unfolds this vast diversity, inclusion, and equity movement. First, servant leadership is criticized for gender bias in its theoretical perspective. Second, it is necessary for management consultants to be aware that servant leadership is criticized as being inapplicable for real-world scenarios.

Knowing this as a management consultant is key to building repertoire. Using the model, as noted, may be risky, but the knowledge gained by knowing this model is crucial to a management consultant's success.

Conclusion

The practicality of the servant leadership model has its roots in helping others and providing hope in an environment that seems to be not only hypercompetitive but also elusive for companies to find a stronghold. Servant leadership is about shifting away from the old paradigm of a hierarchical pyramid-shaped organization, which ignores accountability in the workplace. The new paradigm shift is about taking care of people, all people, and doing so with equity, inclusion, and diversity.

The framework and the key for management consultants is that all leaders should serve their organization to provide the customer and shareholder with the best possible service, but the practicality of the model indicates that servant leadership cannot represent a complete answer to all the needs for leadership in today's global market environment. Thus, the management consultant must be sub-consumed with this reality, and simply present the model as a possible application to leadership development.

The key is to see the model as a catalyst to serve followers and focusing on leadership development to consider serving your organizations and your followers and not anticipate a large change in the leadership gaps that exist in the organization but moving toward a target with a momentum of success in each plateau and throughout the journey to right the wrongs of society and keep an open mind to address them in both the present and future.

Chapter 7

Building a Transactional Leadership Consulting Practice

Being a management consultant automatically makes you a Transactional Leader. Like any consulting capacity, it is a quid per quo type of relationship between the follower and leader. A carrot on the stick approach works at the beginning of the training platform but must be switched as quickly as possible to the participants. The phrase "**carrot on the stick**" is a metaphor for the use of reward and punishment to induce a desired behavior.

When training leaders, the effectiveness of this leadership style is dependent on two conditions. Given that this leadership style may want to be showcased, these are the two premises that must be met:

> *The current differences in organizational hierarchies and structures are totally accepted by subordinates and the second being that all the employees are able to work towards the mutual exchange of benefits where they are rewarded for achieving the goals of the organization.*

This is an important corollary for leaders because It is somewhat reactive just as the transactional leader. The benefit, in the form of a tangible reward, can be held back or taken away if the follower does not achieve the determined goals, but this is somewhat coercive.

Management consultants can reflect on how scholars feel about this leadership theory when presenting it to participants. Reflect on it in a short manner and do this concisely and then move on to the benefits of using Servant

Leadership which was mentioned in the previous chapter.

Scholars look at Transactional Leadership as a passing fancy, a myth, or a schematic diagram that has not been tried and true. Unfortunately for scholars, this is not untried and not untrue. Millions of managers were trained in transactional leadership, and it has advanced into some organization's success----both from a performance level and from management preference.

There is a plethora of leadership theories and models that attempt to consider leadership as an enabler of firm performance. There is an increased emphasis on the important role of leaders when interacting with followers and stakeholders. Transactional leadership involves determining the tasks, rewarding goal achievement, and punishing failure in attaining goals. Transactional leadership style is a new performance paradigm evident in organizations today. Understanding this dimension from a transactional leadership perspective and from a performance paradigm may provide a significant realization of bridging this important field of leadership and management. Transactional leadership is sometimes used with incentives and one executive we trained said that motivation is really "*incentivation*". It works, especially in the short period.

Transactional leadership is successful in developing mutual exchange between leaders and followers. In some instances, this type of leadership may assume impersonal interactions and may not consider higher humanistic desires or relationships between leaders and followers because the nature of the model is to build a transactional agreement on getting tasks done. Interesting enough, this form of leadership is based on grounded theory. While it has its limitations, it is still widely used. This leadership style has been linked with organizational effectiveness, particularly in terms of achieving goals and objectives.

CONCLUSION

The transactional leadership style may appear to posit managers as passive by managing by exception or being laissez-faire when applying leadership. Laissez-faire leaders take a reactive approach to correct mistakes or to overcome problems and laissez-faire leaders do not possess high commitment in seeking the proposed solutions jointly with their subordinates. Transactional leaders rarely consider the empowerment of their followers to assist in problem solving and goal setting. This tenet can be overcome by using a platform that implores leaders to empower followers and engage them in problem solving.

Transactional leadership can be used to review tasks and goals and requirements of subordinates at the beginning of a process such as a fiscal year, new employee orientation, or supervisory development. Leaders would begin using transactional leadership to set goals and determine tasks and then, when time allows, move toward more transformational leadership and place more emphasis on empowered to engage followers.

Another aspect of training with a platform similar to transactional and transformational leadership, is a consulting engagement that supports the McGregor concept of theory X and Y. This leadership approach generates two sides of an X and Y axis. On one side is the concept of leadership that creates change through taking a process-oriented (transactional leadership) and the other as more of a relationship-oriented approach (transformational leadership).

Just as leaders need to be both autocratic and democratic at times, they also need to be both transactional and transformational at times. Knowing these continuums of leadership styles, and also knowing when to use them, and knowing how to use them, is an important concern for management consultants.

Think of transactional leadership as a relationship builder approach in the beginning of any consulting or training endeavor. Then quickly move to more of a transformational style of leadership, training, and consulting. Remember, less hands on and more hands-off training will get management consultants the highest positive rating.

Chapter 8

Building A Culture That Thrives

As a management consultant, you can help executives build an effective company culture to improve customer satisfaction through acquiring additional knowledge from customers, developing better relationships with them, and providing a higher quality of service for them.

When discussing how culture may impact the bottom line with your clients, note that financial performance is determined thorough various aspects such as customer satisfaction. Executives can positively affect financial performance through increased customer satisfaction. Thus, there is a global need to cultivate a strong company culture to accomplish sustainable competitiveness in global markets.

Ed Schein (1985, p.12) describes organizational culture as

> ***"a pattern of shared basic assumptions that the group learned as it solved its problems of external adaptation and internal integration that has worked well enough to be considered valid and, therefore, to be taught to new members as the correct way to perceive, think, and feel in relation to those problems."***

There is a wide platform of contingency training and development when it comes to culture. In fact, every training platform involves changing, improving, or developing an organizational culture. Organizational culture is reflected in shared assumptions, symbols, beliefs, values, and norms that specify how employees understand problems and appropriately react to them (Ogbonna & Harris 2002; Ouchi &

Wilkins 1985; Scott 2003; Smircich 1983; Van Den Berg & Wilderom 2004).

We build our training platform on three dimensions: collaboration, trust, and learning (Lee & Choi 2003). These three cultural aspects play a critical role in improving innovation and enhancing financial performance. For example, collaboration provides a shared understanding about the current issues and problems among employees, which helps to generate new ideas within organizations (Fahey & Prusak 1998; Leonard 1995; Leonard & Sensiper 1998). When employees have trust toward the leader's decisions, this builds a necessary precursor to creating new knowledge and improving financial performance through increased quality of products and services (Lines et al. 2005). Trainers, emphasizing the training platform in real time, consider time spent learning as positively related with the amount of knowledge gained, shared, and implemented, aiming at breaking through performance gaps in corporations. We found that a simple offsite training of three hours in the morning can impact an organization in many positive ways. The sense of camaraderie alone adds value and takes away some of the stress of the day-to-day tasks. Coffee, donuts, and knowledge sharing goes a long way. On the other hand, when an organization does not allow employees to have this free time, it can work in a negative way as participants feel more stressed missing work then learning how to improve it.

As management consultants, we are very involved in

cultural change initiatives and, in particular, by helping executives as decision makers who are responsible for creating a more effective workplace.

Since we specialize in Knowledge Management as a consulting platform, we feel that knowledge, in of itself, is a by-product of culture and culture's role in guiding and facilitating people's action is the key to executive decision-making. By influencing behavior and providing valuable resources, executives can change the culture of an organization (Washington 2008). Management consultants can help executives build a company culture that serves the customer needs, satisfies employees in an equitable way, and helps an organization become more profitable.

There is a competitive advantage for organizations that have strong, cohesive, inclusive cultures because a unique culture is hard for the competition to duplicate.

At the training platform, management consultants can help executives act as change agents who provide a more humanistic and applicable approach to create a great company culture. Executives can facilitate collaboration by developing relationships between, among, and with followers and stakeholders. Emphasizing the need to add the cultural aspect of trust, through considering both employee's individual interests and the organization's essential needs. Emphasizing through leadership development that executives have the capacity to inculcate a culture of trust and transparency of knowledge sharing within organizations so that information can be found and used instantaneously. We encourage participants to identify individual needs and develop a learning culture to generate new knowledge and share it with others instantaneously.

Building a Collaborative Culture

Management consultants can build a collaboration culture. One that has followers actively support and provide significant contributions to each other in the workplace. Our training platform in this area consists of the following:

1. Cohesive culture building to ensure that employees are satisfied by the degree of collaboration between departments, eliminating the silo effect.
2. Developing a culture in which people feel accepted for the way they are and feeling supporting as well as supportive toward others.
3. Exercising a helpful workplace, one in which there is a willingness to help others and accept help when needed and knowing when to seek help.
4. By far the most innovative and creative culture is one that cultivates a sense of misguided effort, there is a willingness to accept responsibility for failure, accept it, and acknowledge failure in a positive way.

Creating a NFTC (No-Fail Trust Culture)

To create a NFTC culture, management consultants can build a platform that helps executives maintain the volume of reciprocal faith in terms of behaviors and intentions. In particular, executives need to build an atmosphere of trust and openness in which:

1. Employees are generally trustworthy of each other, their clients, and the people in their network.
2. Employees have reciprocal faith in other member's intentions and behaviors when it comes to customer service, accepting bribes in some cultures, favors, and perks.
3. Employees have reciprocal faith in the ability of others to carry their weight as part of the team.
4. Employees have reciprocal faith in people's behavior to work toward organizational goals, not only for themselves, but for the good of the organization.
5. Employees have reciprocal faith in people's decisions toward organizational interests that may far succeed their own individual interests.
6. Employees have relationships based on reciprocal faith based upon the handshake, the nod and more importantly, based on someone's word.

Cultivating a Successful Learning Culture

To foster a learning culture, management consultants can build a platform that can help executives enhance the extent to which people are motivated by learning and developing skills within the workplace. Once introduced to a learning environment, executives can contribute to the development of learning:

1. Various formal training programs through webinars, guest speakers, experts, break-out groups, offsite excursions are provided to improve cultural and work performance.
2. Opportunities for informal individual development other than formal training such as work assignments and job rotation and increased responsibility in both depth and breadth of one's career can enhance job design.
3. Funding the opportunity to encourage external seminars, conferences, licensing, certification, and symposia expands learning and development.
4. Provide the opportunity to form various social mechanisms such as clubs and community gatherings that enhance camaraderie.
5. Encourage employee feedback on how satisfied they are by the contents of job training or self-development programs.
6. Develop career placement and development with a rotation among products, services, and departments to build a thorough knowledge base for employees.

CONCLUSION

This chapter inspires leaders to embrace culture so that

they can create fundamental change that impacts diversity, equity, and inclusion. Organizational culture has risen to an all-time high with the debilitating pandemic of 2020 to 2022, increased remote work, and the great resignation.

From the wisdom of Ed Schein to the creative genius of Jim Clawson, building a collaborative culture is by far a core competitive advantage. The questions executives need to answer are how people feel when coming and going to work, what do they say about their workplace, are they advocates for the organization, and are they truly happy with their career. Failure to address anyone of these questions may lead to a weak cultural environment.

Consultants expressing the term failure must address it without the notion of it happening yet preparing for it, recognizing it early, and creating solutions to address it if it occurs. Cohesiveness can be built with a strong culture to address issues as they arise and not be reactive too late. Creating a no-fail trust-culture will assure both innovation and creativity. There is also the possibility of defectors when trusting people and accepting failure. People will leave for competitors and take their ideas to a more rewarding, accepting, and trusting culture.

While working as an executive for Salomon Brothers in Tampa, Florida in the 90s, a whole trading desk left Raymond James and joined Salomon because there was a lack of trust, innovative acceptance, and initiative. Jamie Dimon, at J.P. Morgan was paid 20 million dollars to not take any of his followers for two years when he left a Wall Street investment bank.

Learning cultures are extremely important for yuppies (Young Up and Coming Executives), but even seasoned executives need training and development. At minimum, they need the opportunity to attend conferences, ascertain certifications, and be knowledgeable about new innovations and technology.

Several practices mentioned in this chapter can represent a complete platform for management consultants when training executives to that they can create cultural change initiatives in today's global market environment. Thus, go out and be the innovator, creator, and facilitator of a cohesive culture and meet the stakeholder's needs so that they can become advocates of the organization.

Chapter 9

The Right Corporate Structure Formula

Flexible corporate structures are more equipped to succeed in our global business environment. These types of structures inspire innovation and creativity.

Corporate structure has been defined as a pattern by which organizations can divide their activities and tasks as well as control them to achieve higher degrees of coordination. Corporate structure, therefore, refers to the bureaucratic division of labor accompanied by control and coordination between different tasks in order to develop communication within organizations.

Consultants will find two types of structures that stand out among the majority of organizations. One being a centralization or formalization which may be the most common structural aspect to examine corporate structure. This type of structure may inhibit risk taking which may inspire employees to take risk-related efforts and generate more innovative solutions. To examine centralization, executives should explore the degree of control and authority over decisions in hierarchical levels. Formalization, as another structural aspect, is operationally investigated through measuring the extent to which working relationships and decisions are assigned by formal language that represents official statements, policies, rules, and procedures. Both of these corporate structures are somewhat rigid, but they still work and are used throughout the world.

It is important for management consultants to understand that corporate structure can be reshaped by executives when they develop knowledge sharing and inspire employees to create new ideas for a better environment among business-units and departments. The informal structure could facilitate new idea generation to build a more innovative climate within organizations. Management consultants can particularly help executives to implement organizational changes that develop better collaboration among subordinates and managers.

The management consultant will have clients in both the centralized and decentralized culture and training for these organizations has to be somewhat different. When training in a centralized culture, the management consultant will provide a more canned and approved training. With decentralized training, the consultant can take more liberty in the presentation and delivery of the training.

We experienced a centralized training culture in which we pitched a one-hour training with the intention of conducting a half-day to full-day training. The boss was so rigid that he wanted to review the entire PowerPoint. Once approved, he did not expect any changes. We took the liberty to make a minor change on one of the power point slides and this cost us the gig. Thus, the rigidity of the centralized structure has to keep the approved training platform fully approved and delivered that way. Any deviation can cost you the gig.

Decision making is probably the most notable difference between the centralized versus decentralized culture. Scholars found that more emphasis on formalized and mechanistic structures can negatively impact the executive's ability to exert such change while a more decentralized and flexible structure may improve departmental and managerial interactions. The reasoning behind this claim is that the mechanical or centralization at the commanding level of leadership impairs the opportunity to develop relationships among managers, business units, and departments.

Management consultants should be aware that executives can reshape corporate structure to be more effective when the command center of organizations can disseminate information in a decentralized and organic way as opposed to the mechanical and centralized command center.

Decentralized structures shift the power of decision-making to the lower levels and subsequently inspire organizational members to create new ideas and even implement them while centralized structures may negatively impact interdepartmental communications and inhibit knowledge exchange.

A more decentralized and flexible structure may enable executives to improve departmental and managerial interactions that can lead to identifying the best opportunities for investment that may potentially lead to improved knowledge utilization processes for companies.

Knowledge utilization process can positively contribute to knowledge management through building more decentralized structures within organizations. When training, the consultant can facilitate knowledge management through developing a more flexible structure that is considered an essential source for developing relationships. Consultants need to facilitate more and lecture less. This is hard for some consultants that like the stage and feel that they have a lot of experience and knowledge to offer. The key is to get the participants to talk more and facilitate more and encourage more participation. Content trainers are paid less then management consultants that inspire more with less content.

When we develop our cultural aspects in our training sessions, we focus on knowledge management because we feel that it is a significant indicator of improving organizational performance. Knowledge management can, in fact, improve organizational performance through increasing sales, enhancing customer satisfaction, developing new novel learning opportunities, encouraging innovation, and improving the quality of products and services. This enhances the shareholder and stakeholders relationship and they become organizational advocates.

We train executives to have a flexible corporate structure that links knowledge management and firm performance together to serve the customer needs and help the organization become more profitable. On occasion, we find that the corporate structure is not completely in favor of supporting knowledge management, and in these instances, we have found that executives cannot effectively manage organizational knowledge to improve performance.

The key kernel for management consultants is that

corporate structure is a resource that enables organizations to solve problems and create value through improved performance and it is this point that will narrow the gaps of success and failure leading to more successful decision-making.

Flexible structures can directly impact leadership effectiveness, especially during a turbulent environment. In this structure, leaders inspire followers to generate new solutions to create a better work environment to offset turbulence.

A highly centralized structure may have a negative impact on leadership practices because rigidity brings with it stress and, in some cases, monotony.

While decentralization positively contributes to executives in developing a more innovative climate, this enhanced decentralized structure facilitates the exchange of ideas and the implementation of more innovative solutions based on the power of decision-making at all levels of the organization, especially the front line which has a direct impact with customers in many cases.

Thus, highly formalized structures are more bureaucratic, and this negatively contributes to the effectiveness of leadership in changing the existing troubled situations and creating a better culturally satisfying environment. An environment that serves the lower echelon of the organization just as much as it serves the top executives.

Conclusion

Management consultants can help reshape corporate structure to develop a more flexible corporate structure that provides open access to knowledge and information. We suggest that flexible structures constitute the foundation of a supportive workplace to disseminate knowledge and subsequently enhance overall organizational performance.

We highlight some beneficial managerial implications for management consultants and industry leaders. In addition, we extend the current literature by showing how management consultants can help executive enhance leadership effectiveness by reshaping corporate structure to capture the voice of the employer.

Chapter 10

How to Succeed in Strategy Consulting?

Most organizations plan well into the future. Strategic goals spanning five to fifteen years is usually the norm. Short-term goals are more tactical and are just as important, and in some cases, they take precedence during turbulent times. Two prominent strategic management scholars by the names of Hofer and Schendel (1978) see strategy as a "fundamental pattern of present and planned resource deployments and environmental interactions that indicates how the organization will achieve its objectives." Andrew (1971) describes strategy as a pattern of decisions and plans which are directed at interacting with the external and internal environment and effectively and efficiently allocating capabilities to achieve organizational objectives. Rumelt (1979) shows that strategy primarily aims to develop goals and plans to restructure unclear and vague situations into a set of organizationally resolvable problems. As a result, strategy is formed to efficiently deploy capabilities and interact with environments which are both internal and external. There are different typologies of strategies, one can create better results when they are based upon prior experience. New organizations do not have this luxury and it is the management consultant that can steer them in the correct direction.

Venkatraman (1989), an author and scholar in the area of strategic management at Boston University concentrates on the dimensions of corporate strategy, and recommends the four strategic dimensions of analysis, pro-activeness, defensiveness, and futurity. Analysis strategy is defined, by Venkatraman (1989), as the tendency to search for problems and their root cause and then generates better alternatives to solve them. When executives analyze strategy, they can create more knowledge and find the best solution using a problematic search of various options. This type of strategy formulation stimulates companies to apply information systems in their decision-making processes in order to investigate various alternatives and options (Morgan & Strong, 2003). Also, executives analyze strategic milestones to meet the goals of employee development. Analysis strategy can develop opportunities for employee development through assessing current situations in detail (Zheng, Yang & McLean, 2010).

This type of strategy provides new and more innovative solutions for organizational problems as they arise. To develop this strategy, management consultants can particularly help client organizations develop a workplace in which they:

1. Provide emphasis on the effective coordination among different functional areas.

2. Use extensive information systems to support decision making.
3. Add comprehensive analysis undertaken when confronted with an important decision.
4. Use planning techniques.
5. Create effective deployment of management information and control systems.
6. Use manpower planning and performance appraisal of senior managers.

Pro-activeness is a strategy element used by executives who take a proactive approach to search for better positions in the business environment (Talke, 2007; Gilbert & Reid, 2009). As executives use the pro-activeness strategy which refers to finding new opportunities and proactively responding to current challenges in external environments, they can enhance their span of control. To cultivate a pro-activeness strategy, management consultants can particularly help client organizations develop a workplace in which they:

1. Provide a constant search for new opportunities.
2. Attempt to introduce new brands or products in the market in a timely manner.
3. Search for businesses that can be acquired.
4. Create more effective expansion of capacity when compared to competitors.
5. Examine strategic elimination of those operations that

are no longer profitable in the later stages of product and organizational life cycles.

Defensiveness strategic elements recommend undertaking defensive behaviors that manifest themselves in enhancing efficiency and in cutting costs while maintaining continuous budget-analysis and break-even points (Bergeron, Raymond & Rivard, 2004; Zheng, 2005). Executives can take an offensive approach, and, in this case, they employ a defensive strategy. A defensive strategy utilizes modifications in order to use organizational resources, decrease costs, and control operational risk efficiently and effectively (Karabulut, 2015). Some executives feel that a defensive strategy, while necessary, sets a negative connotation on their span of control. On the contrary, a defensiveness strategic approach, in fact, enhances organizational learning through reusing commercial knowledge (Venkatraman, 1989). To foster this strategy, management consultants can particularly help client organizations develop a workplace in which they:

1. Set up regular modifications to the manufacturing/service technology.
2. Use cost control systems for monitoring performance.
3. Use current management techniques to ensure that they move smoothly at the required level of competitiveness.
4. Pace emphasis on product and service quality through

the use of work improvement teams.

Futurity is reflected in the degree to which the strategic decision-making process takes a two-way approach----an emphasis on both long-term effectiveness and shorter-term efficiency concurrently (Kazaz & Ulubeyli, 2009). Executives use futurity strategy to expand the growth opportunities available to companies to close the gap between success and failure. Futurity strategy implements basic studies to identify and actively respond to the changes occurred in the external environment and provides better outcomes (Venkatraman, 1989). To create a futurity strategy, management consultants can particularly help client organizations develop a workplace in which they:

1. Create specific criteria that is used for resource allocation which generally reflect short-term considerations.
2. Place emphasis on basic research to provide them with a competitive edge for the future.
3. Recognize key indicators of operational forecasting.
4. Design a system for formal tracking of significant and general trends.
5. Develop regular analyses of critical issues and address them accordingly.

Conclusion

This chapter summarizes the information needed to be successful using the black box of management consultants and executives worldwide. The key is for executives to consider channeling organizational processes into corporate strategy and employ a supportive strategy that executives can continue to prosper and grow. Success is dependent upon how executives formulate and execute corporate strategy.

Management consultants can see how they can help client's cultivate an effective corporate strategy, which can enable superior performance to achieve business objectives and satisfy not only their stakeholders but also their own organizations progress and success.

Chapter 11

Becoming a Knowledge Management Consultant

This chapter finds you either already a management consultant or aspiring to become one. Whether you are a seasoned consultant or you are new to the field, this chapter offers a wealth of knowledge to add to your black box.

Management consultants must understand how knowledge can be categorized. There are two important taxonomies of knowledge that need to be discussed. Management consultants can capitalize not only their knowledge but also on the knowledge management of the organization's already established knowledge in which they facilitate.

Human, Social, and Structured Knowledge

Two scholars by the name of Long and Fahey (2000) argue that knowledge can also be classified using individual, social, and structured dimensions. Executives can categorize followers based on their human knowledge which focuses on individual knowledge and manifests itself in individual's competencies and skills. This type of knowledge includes both tacit and explicit knowledge. Long and Fahey (2000) suggest that this form of knowledge comprises the skills gained by individual experiences and learned as rules and instructions formulated by executives for followers to use as a guide. Social knowledge, on the other hand, is categorized as tacit knowledge that is shared so that it can become collective knowledge. Executives can use structured knowledge that emerges in formal language from annual reports, memos, and other means of communication to be represented as statements and is considered explicit knowledge. Therefore, consultants can classify knowledge in this way so that it emerges at three levels----individual (i.e., human), group (i.e., social), and organizational (i.e., structured).

Scientific, Philosophical, and Commercial Knowledge

There is a scientific, philosophical, and commercial side to knowledge that consultants should at least be aware of in today's hypercompetitive business environment. Demarest (1997), divides knowledge into these three categories. Scientific knowledge is objective and manifests itself as provable and verifiable knowledge or truth, while philosophical knowledge clarifies that "truth is embedded in language and therefore inaccessible" (Demarest 1997, p.375). The key for consultants is that knowledge as per Demarest (1997, p.375), especially commercial knowledge, unlike scientific and philosophical knowledge, focuses on enhancing "effective performance." Answering the questions consultants often ask: "What works, or so what?" Based on this view, this kind of knowledge empowers the capabilities of an organization, and actively improves its competitive advantage in the marketplace. Consultants are aware that commercial knowledge takes an objective approach and can positively contribute to a firm's performance. The key is how to use this knowledge, enhance it, distribute it, and capture it.

Facilitating Knowledge Management

Executives today are more focused on strategic management decision making due to the hypercompetitive global environment and the public and private sector evaluation and opinion. Public organizations are attempting to function as private profit-wise while public companies have the Wall Street analysts continuously evaluating their strategic moves. Lee and Kim's (2001) model for managing knowledge takes a strategic process-oriented approach and is relevant to executive leadership. It is important for management consultants to build a climate of openness for individuals to exchange ideas. Knowledge is accumulated by creating new approaches to gathering, evaluating, and disseminating information throughout the organizations.

Consultants need to make deliberate attempts to inspire people to create new ideas and develop effective mechanisms to acquire knowledge from various sources such as suppliers, customers, business partners, and competitors. This is similar to a value-chain approach. Consultants should support this approach because they play a strategic role in expanding the knowledge accumulation through applying incentives as mechanisms to develop a more innovative climate. The importance is to manage effective tools to acquire knowledge from external sources.

Consultants should integrate knowledge internally to enhance the workplace. We find that the best to build a skill is to apply it right away to test it out and tweak it with the consultant's own style. Knowledge integration focuses on monitoring and controlling knowledge management practices, evaluating the effectiveness of current knowledge, defining and recognizing core knowledge areas, coordinating expert opinions, sharing organizational knowledge, and scanning for new knowledge to keep the quality of products or services continuously improving. Consultants can promote knowledge integration by creating expert groups or steering committees to enhance knowledge quality and evaluate knowledge.

Follower's diversity of skills and interpersonal relations, that is usually based on trust and reciprocity can improve the performance of group cohesiveness. In the process of knowledge integration, knowledge provides valuable contributions to products and services.

Consultants should have the desirable expertise to steer the organizational strategy and facilitate this process by undertaking initiatives that improve knowledge transfer. Thus, enhancing the performance of employees and the implementation of effective change to maintain the quality of products and services.

The burden of success when effective implementation of knowledge integration is concerned is heavily dependent on the capabilities of the organization's management consultant.

Furthermore, it is important for management consultants to reconfigure organizational knowledge. When executives agree to share knowledge with other organizations in the environment, studies have shown that knowledge is often difficult to share externally (Zehua, 2012; Jianbin et al., 2014). One reason for this is that other organizations have too much pride to accept new knowledge or are apprehensive to expose themselves to the competition. Therefore, executives may lack the required capabilities to interact with other organizations, or distrust sharing their knowledge. In addition, just the notion of creating an expert group or steering committee may be shortsighted because such groups may not have sufficient backgrounds and experiences to comprehend knowledge acquired from external sources. Many consultants are aware of networking with business partners which is a key activity for organizations to enhance knowledge exchange.

Networking is a critical concern for management consultants in the process of developing alliances with partners in external environments and helping participants meet others that may help them too. I always open up my seminars with is anyone in need of work today; and, then I follow up with, is anyone hiring? Direct match up of encouragement. It worked like a charm.

Executives and their expert groups or steering

committees are important to make the final decisions about developing alliances with business partners.

Consultants, therefore, should understand what it is about the organization's capabilities that allow the organization to develop alliances with business partners and interact with other organizations.

Management consultants across the globe have found that knowledge is critical to business success. Knowledge, in and of itself, is not enough to satisfy the vast array of changes in today's organization. However, knowledge management is the only necessary precursor to effectively managing knowledge within the organization. First management consultants should understand the concept of knowledge itself.

Knowledge is identified as a multi-faceted concept, and is distinct from information and data (Alavi & Leidner, 2001; Grover & Davenport, 2001). Data has been defined as raw entities, and information is understood as a meaningful pattern within these raw entities (Bell, 1999; Tsoukas & Vladimirou, 2001; Wiseman, 2008). In Beckman's (1999) view, knowledge can be categorized using two approaches:

- One being that knowledge can be understood as a concept for solving problems. Based on this approach, Bock (2001) evaluates knowledge as a combination of rules, procedures, beliefs and

skills that positively contribute to solving organizational problems.
- The second approach views knowledge as "truths and beliefs, perspectives and concepts, judgments and expectation methodologies, and know-how" (Wiig, 1993, p. p.73).

These definitions are still not enough for management consultants because knowledge is quite elusive and is changing on a day-to-day basis with discontinued products and the ever-changing vast array of technology.

Therefore, to counter the above definition of knowledge, Ruggles (1997) defines knowledge as a blend of information, experiences and codes, while Amidon (1997) argues that knowledge is a collection of meaningful information.

One scholar that is well known in the Academy of Management, one of the largest leadership and management organizations in the world by the name of Peter Senge (1997) highlights the importance of knowledge for organizations. Senge (1997), nominated one of the foremost thought leaders in management, says that successful organizations enhance their competitiveness by focusing on learning. Another scholar with over 40 books by the name of Drucker (1998, p.17), comments that "the productivity of knowledge and knowledge workers will not be the only competitive factor in the world economy. It is, however, likely to become the decisive factor, at least for most industries in the developed countries."

Management consultants should read Drucker's work because it is directly applied to managerial decision making.

The key take-away for management consultants is that knowledge management is a resource that enables organizations to solve problems and create value through improved competitive performance and it is this point that will narrow the gaps of success and failure leading to more successful decision-making (Argote & Ingram, 2000; Truch, 2001; Award & Ghaziri, 2004).

Knowledge Management Development

Management consultants are perplexed by the amount, both depth and breadth, of knowledge management models and applications. A new model that can easily be applied that takes into consideration some of the major tasks that management consultants must consider is needed in the extant literature. Management consultants can look at a three step processes of knowledge accumulation, integration, and reconfiguration (Lee & Kim, 2001).

The following Figure 1 depicts our knowledge management model. The key point in this model is the knowledge accumulation section coupled with integration and reconfiguration to ensure that the knowledge is actually helping organizations grow both professionally for individuals and profitably for all stakeholders.

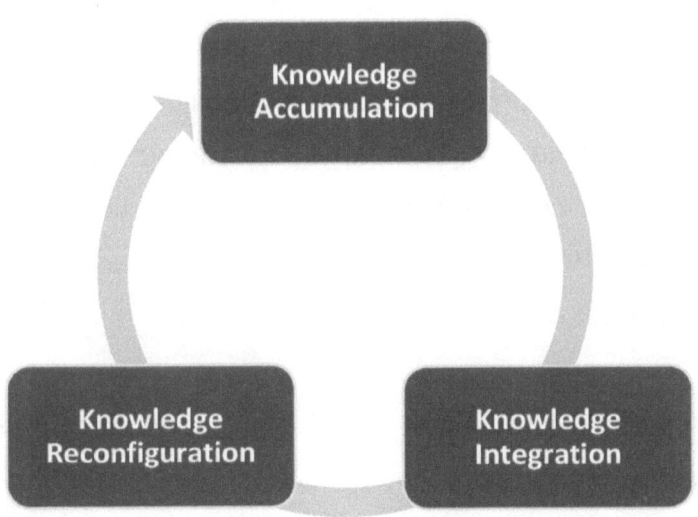

Figure 1: Knowledge Management Model

Quadrant 1 - Knowledge Accumulation

The knowledge accumulation process in this model plays an important role for organizations through acquiring knowledge and information from the external business environment and developing the capabilities to create new knowledge within a company. In doing this process, management consultants can help executives and organizations develop a workplace which is effective in the following areas:

- Acquiring knowledge about new products and services within the industry.
- Benchmarking performance with competitors in their industry.
- Using feedback to improve subsequent practices.
- Utilizing teams (e.g., committees or management teams) to manage knowledge resources.
- Developing and implementing education or training programs.

- Carrying out a career path program or recruitment program to acquire experts.
- Conducting organizational events (such as a "knowledge contests" or "knowledge fairs") that promote knowledge activities to innovate and create new products and services.

Quadrant 2 - Knowledge Integration

A further step to implementing knowledge management is to integrate knowledge within organizations. The key here is to internally integrate knowledge so that it is quickly retrievable at the right time and place. Knowledge cannot be used adequately if it takes time to acquire it. Expert systems can provide kiosks that are knowledge databanks and intranet searches to retrieve information from the knowledge bank quickly and effectively. In doing this process, management consultants can help executives and organizations develop a workplace which is effective in the following areas:

- Monitoring or controlling organizational knowledge to keep products and services in line with market requirements.
- Regularly assessing knowledge requirements according to environmental changes.
- Linking the knowledge sharing system using various software and programs.

- Defining "core knowledge" or "core competence" areas.
- Using expert groups to evaluate the quality and effectiveness of organizational knowledge.
- Disseminating organizational knowledge among employees.
- Rewarding individuals or teams based on the quality of the knowledge generated.

Quadrant 3 - Knowledge Reconfiguration

Moreover, competing organizations find ways to share common knowledge so that it can be used by industry alliance when the information is non-specific to a certain organization. Organizations must collaborate with other companies and share their knowledge with them to improve community issues and global problems in a manner that solves problems and creates solutions when necessary. This is called knowledge reconfiguration. The key kernel for management consultants is that knowledge is shared with other organizations to recognize the changes occurring in external environments and respond to them quickly and effectively. In doing this process, management consultants can help executives and organizations develop a workplace which is effective in the following areas:

- Creating knowledge alliances with suppliers, customers, or other partners.
- Sharing knowledge management visions and goals with external partners (such as suppliers and customers or other partners) to develop collaborative activities, shared goals and trust-based relationships with them.
- Extending (or linking) knowledge related policies or rules (measurement, rewards) with external partners (such as customers, suppliers or other partners).
- Linking their knowledge sharing system with external partners (such as customers, suppliers or other partners).
- Facilitating and implementing activities such as conferences, contests, and seminars with external partners.

Conclusion

In this chapter, we place a new emphasis on the "how" of knowledge management development within organizations using new tools that can added to the black box.

Management consultants accumulate knowledge by integrating it into day-to-day operations. A continuous reconfiguration of knowledge develops when executives are trained to recognize the changes occurring in external environments and respond to them quickly and effectively.

Thus, it is imperative that the management consultant stay abreast on the news of the day so that they can help executives implement this knowledge.

The knowledge management model expressed in this chapter takes a task-based approach by translating the management of knowledge into a complete set of processes. Processes that can make or break an organization. Consult with this model and your management consultant practice will be a great success.

Chapter 12

Managing Risk Requires a Knowledge-Based Approach

Consultants are spending more time today concerned about operational risk management than ever before. Consultants that manage operational risk and use it as an important driving force for business success find their clients to be more competitive and on the cutting edge. Operational risk management has been developed to offset problems before they occur and to adjust or shift resources accordingly in the event of a threat or risk.

Operational risk management is an operational approach to represent knowledge management and seeks to apply organizational knowledge in order to effectively manage the risks associated with running a successful consulting project for a client (Keskin 2005). Similar to customer relationship management (CRM), knowledge management is an enabler for identifying and satisfying customer's needs and CRM manifests itself as a significant driver that motivates the development of relationships with customers (Hu et al. 1997).

As mentioned in the previous chapter, scholars have proven that consultants can use knowledge management to improve customer satisfaction through acquiring additional knowledge from customers, developing better relationships with them, and providing a higher quality of consulting services for them (North, Reinhardt & Schmidt, 2004; Sukumaran et al. 2009).

The key function of knowledge management is to help consultants use it for employee development and training (Spender, 1996). In this context, training is becoming the forefront of business success worldwide. The reason for this is because learning is a process that leads to acquiring new insights and knowledge, and potentially corrects sub-optimal or ineffective actions and behaviors that cause consulting projects to spiral out of control (Dorfler, 2010).

Consultants have found that organizational learning modifies behaviors resulting in newer insight and knowledge (Aulakh et al., 2016). Thus, the changing of the existing behaviors of followers and by generating new knowledge is a key factor in improving competitive advantage (Linderman et al. 2004).

Our experience indicates that management consultants can add more manageable control and private knowledge not to be shared with competitors and this reduces operational risk. Private knowledge refers to "a resource that is valuable, rare, and imperfectly imitable," and therefore is regarded as "firm-specific" (Matusik 1998, p.683). Unique strategies, processes, and practices are examples of this type of knowledge. This type of knowledge in consulting projects must be guarded and not shared with the competition. Any leak of such information may increase the operational risk. Contrary to private knowledge, public knowledge differs in that it is not unique for any consulting project (Matusik 1998). Public knowledge may be an asset and provide potential benefits when posted in social media and other means of communication. Consultants package knowledge and use it for an entire industry. According to Matusik (1998, p.683), public knowledge has been defined as "industry and occupational best practices" and is reflected in various concepts such as total quality management, six-sigma, the Malcolm Baldridge Award, and just-in-time inventory.

It is important for consultants to consider the ownership of knowledge as a factor which is a significant contributor to the knowledge of consulting projects. Moreover, Matusik (1998) points out that knowledge emerges in two additional forms, including the knowledge that is only accessible by one organization and the knowledge that is accessible to all. The best approach to manage knowledge when training is for consultants to know which knowledge is to remain private and which knowledge is approved for participants to go public with. A mistake in this area may be vital to the consulting projects and consultants must choose wisely.

Furthermore, internal resources manifest themselves in tangible (such as physical properties and machinery) and intangible (such as intellectual capital) forms. Intangible resources, in form of intellectual capital, exist primarily as knowledge in human resources and cannot be easily imitated. This, by far, is why some consulting projects are successful and some are not. The operational risk of consulting projects may be at risk if they can be easily imitated by the competition. Therefore, decreasing the imitability of products and services can also decrease the operational risk. Thus, making products and services harder to copy or imitate.

To remain competitive, consultants should realize that they have to quickly create and share new ideas and knowledge to be more responsive to market changes (Eisenhardt & Santos, 2006). Consulting teams are "social communities that specialize in the creation and internal transfer of knowledge" (Kogut & Zander, 1993 p.625). Importantly, knowledge held by members is the most strategic resource for competitive advantage. The way it is managed by consultants is imperative (Kogut & Zander, 1992; De Carolis, 2002; Curado, 2006).

Knowledge improves operational risk management, and potentially limits potential operational risk. In particular, knowledge-based risk management develops cohesive infrastructures to store and retrieve knowledge to enable clients by effectively using organizational resources, decreasing costs, and creating more innovative solutions. Thus, when consultants ensure the effectiveness of knowledge management, they increase control and lessen operational risk. As a result, it is safe to say that private knowledge is essential for consulting projects while knowledge management, if not embraced, can lead to operational risk.

There is a gap in the management literature toward identifying the catalysts of social capital in organizations. The question arises: *How can management consultants affect company characteristics to build social capital?* This basic question remained unexplored since the inception of the social capital theory to date. To address this gap, we indicate how the three important dimensions of social capital theory (structural, cognitive, and relational) are affected by various internal characteristics of companies such as the structure, the culture, the strategy, the inter-company networks, and the stakeholder orientation. The significance of our strategic tenets and networking suggestions relate to social capital theory. A renowned management theory that management should know.

We present a theoretical framework that incorporates the organizational factors that may impact the three dimensions of social capital. The literature, to date, has failed to provide a comprehensive framework which incorporates all of the contextual factors that may simultaneously impact social capital. The absence of this systematic approach inhibits the development of social capital as a vital driver of business success. Exploring these organizational factors and how they may impact offers practical implications for management consultants to improve outcomes at the organizational level and meet business objectives.

Building Social Capital

Social capital stresses the critical role that executives place on relationships (Claudia, Brock & Shaw 2017). Social capital is different from human capital in that human capital focuses on individual behavior and knowledge while social capital emphasizes relationships and the assets created by these relationships (Claudia, Brock & Shaw 2017). By viewing employees as assets, organizations are treating human capital as individual quality. Social capital is considered the quality that appears in interactions throughout the organization, not individually.

Management consultants may not be as interested in social capital as much as scholars are but there is a kernel worth looking it in this theory for management consultants. For example, social capital increases organizational performance and helps close the gap between success and possible failure.

Nahapiet and Ghoshal (1998) determine three dimensions for social capital, and categorize them as structural, cognitive, and relational. The structural dimension actually portrays an overall pattern of connections among actors (Choi 2002). This dimension could possibly be improved by having access to other actors quickly and enhanced through highly flexible structures.

Two scholars by the names of Wang and Ahmed (2003) indicate that highly flexible structures such as organic structures may be prone to better socialization among organizational departments and business units. These scholars also indicate that structural aspects of formalization and centralization may negatively relate to structural dimension of social capital theory. Therefore, management consultants can affect a firm's structure (i.e., formalization and centralization) to help create a more decentralized and organic structure that facilitates social capital to conform to the needs and expectations of strategic goals and objectives.

The cognitive dimension is also defined as resources developing shared vision, interpretations and feelings among actors (Nahapiet, & Ghoshal 1998). Similarly, Schein (1985, p.12), one of the most prominent management scholars, defines organizational culture as "the correct way to perceive, think, and feel" in order to solve organizational problems. Putnam, Leonardi and Nanetti (1993, p. 171) found that "trust is an essential component of social capital," and argue that trust enhances interactions among employees. In agreement, Villalonga-Olives and Kawachi (2015) consider trust as an important facilitator of social capital.

The link presupposed here provides significant evidence that social capital requires cooperation, and cooperation demands collaborative behaviors. Furthermore,

Avila Cobo (2005, p.18) argues that collaboration is a strong determinant of "the very existence, the strength, and the durability of social capital."

Thus, cognitive dimension seeks to achieve a shared vision. Shared vision is a mutual understanding toward determined goals, and this common perception could be reached through developing learning opportunities. Therefore, cultural aspects of trust, collaboration, and learning may be positively associated with the cognitive dimension of social capital theory. Hence, management consultants can reshape organizational culture (i.e., trust, collaboration, and learning) to create social capital within departmental and business units of organizations.

Another important component, the relational dimension focuses on the importance of relations, and argues that relations based on obligations, reciprocity and identification could develop organizational assets. Nahapiet and Ghoshal (1998, p. 255) define obligations as "a commitment or duty to undertake some activity in the future." Sort of a due diligence of each employee to put in the necessary effort to help the organization prosper.

In order for a company to prosper, management consultants must develop a strong organizational strategy. Organizational strategy is evaluated as "a plan for interacting with competitive environments to achieve organizational goals" (Lyonga 2017, p. 34).

Strategy highlights the critical role of relations with external actors and enhances social interactions with business units and the organizational environment in order to attain goals in the future. Furthermore, organizational strategy develops a shared interpretation among organizational members and positively relates to the cognitive dimension of social capital theory. Organizational strategy can be, therefore, positively connected to cognitive and relational dimensions of social capital theory.

Reciprocity, another aspect worth noting, stresses upon helping behavior and knowledge contribution between resources and recipients. Inter-company networks are a key part of this relationship and play a critical role in enhancing knowledge transference among people. Two scholars by the names of Ostrom and Ahn (2003) illustrate that inter-company networks are a crucial condition for reciprocity and highlight the importance of inter-company networks in creating reciprocity.

Furthermore, one scholar, that is well known in the Academy of Management, one of the largest leadership and management organizations in the world, by the name of Coleman (1988) argues that inter-company networks facilitate access to other people and resources, and this could improve structural social capital which is highly affected by having access to other people quickly.

Therefore, it may be established that inter-corporate networks have a positive relationship with relational and structural social capital. This idea is capsulized by Putnam (2000, p.19) who states that "the core idea of social capital theory is that networks have value." Thus, It can be argued that management consultants can positively contribute to social capital through building inter-corporate networks.

The stakeholder orientation is about enhancing the exchange of knowledge with various stakeholders. Much of the knowledge exchanged with stakeholders is a result of social interactions between organizations and their stakeholders. Another prominent scholar on social capital theory is Cots (2011) who affirms the critical role of social capital and highlights a strong association between the dimensions of social capital and stakeholder orientation.

We depict that the three dimensions of social capital emerge in social interactions with stakeholders. Management consultants should establish a stakeholder orientation because this may be positively related to all the three dimensions of social capital. Therefore, factors affecting social capital are depicted in the following figure and we offer this framework as part of the management consultant's black box.

Figure 1: Organizational Resources and Social Capital

Conclusion

This chapter contributes to management consulting practice by identifying the ways in which management consultants can build social capital in organizations.

We provide elaborative insights for management consultants by modeling how the three dimensions of social capital theory can be affected by organizational characteristics such as the structure, the culture, the strategy, the inter-company networks, and most importantly, the stakeholder orientation.

The three dimensions of structural, cognitive, and relational social capital is enhanced with our model.

This chapter develops management consultant's understanding of the direct impact of company characteristics on social capital. Management consultants can build social capital through affecting organizational factors.

Thus, management consultants can manifest themselves as change agents who have developed competencies to better manage organizational factors with the aim of fostering social capital in client's companies.

Chapter 13

A New Path to Organizational Knowledge Management

We found three things that leaders are focusing on during the post-pandemic period. The executives we contacted told us that they are focusing on transformational leadership, knowledge management, and information technology, We contacted executives that were leading during the post-pandemic period, and they have noted that the post-pandemic recover requires effective technological infrastructure that are developed to monitor and sustain competitive advantage concurrently.

During the post-pandemic period, executives are striving to meet the customer needs while maintaining employee satisfaction levels and stockholder equity. In some cases, downsizing was kept to a minimum at that time, but now, in January 2023, downsizing may be on the rise. According to business insider, reporters by the name of Avery Hartmans, Samantha Delouya, and Bethany Biron updated the current state of layoffs on Dec 26, 2022:

> *"Goldman Sachs plans to cut thousands of workers. Here are the other major US companies that have made cuts in 2022, from Amazon to*

Twitter. A wave of layoffs has swept across American businesses in 2022. The cuts stem from slower business growth, paired with rising labor costs. The layoffs span across industries, from mortgage lending to digital-payment processing."

While executives being trained by consultants must be prepared to update their resumes, there are a cadre of implications to be addressed when consulting about career planning, career development, and career consulting.

For example, strategic objectives are key to success if they counteract the demise of supplier support and vendor relationships as the world manages the pandemic. The primary function of knowledge management is to restructure unclear and vague situations into a set of organizationally resolvable problems. The pandemic evolves around the most hypercompetitive pressure from both internal and external sources as a result, knowledge management is implemented formed to efficiently deploy the organizational capabilities and help organizations interact with environments.

Executives are also setting goals that are realistic and specific but leave room for change and adaptation so that the goals are not so rigid. They have expressed that leader possessing the skills of transformational leadership engage in the facilitation of achieving more sustainable changes in organizations. When training executives, we ask the following vital questions:

- How does transformational leadership impact knowledge management?
- How can the better use of information technology mediate the relationship between transformational leadership and knowledge management?

Transformational leadership plays a vital role in leading technological changes to better manage organizational knowledge. A systematic approach toward transformational leadership as a significant indicator of managing technology and improving knowledge management processes can provide practical guidelines for management executives. In addition, developing a new and dynamic conception of transformational leadership within the information technology and knowledge management paradigms can propel leaders into the post-pandemic world in which they now engage.

Organizations such as Zoom, WebEx, and Microsoft Teams led the way for the remote worker.

Theoretical Insight Into The Post-COVID World

To best describe the actions necessary to handle to tumultuous post-pandemic, we emphasize importance of the knowledge-based view. Our reasoning is that more so today then pre-pandemic times, organizations exist as social communities designed to enhance competitive advantage by utilizing and creating new ideas and knowledge. Knowledge creation and utilization manifest themselves as constructs of the knowledge-based view (Zheng, 2005; Zheng, Yang, & Mclean, 2010).

The knowledge-based view focuses on embedding knowledge in organizational members, and accordingly, uncovers tacit knowledge embedded within employees as a more important source of competitive advantage than explicit knowledge (Reus, 2004; Darroch, 2005; Wu, & Chen, 2014). With remote work still vibrant, sitting behind a computer has now become the norm and technology has enhanced the platform of survival. In fact, information technology affecting competitive advantage through enabling knowledge within organizations present itself as an internal resource. Thus, working remotely, can be controlled by organizations effectively. However, we have found that both effectiveness and efficiency are tantamount, and organizations cannot survive the post-pandemic without both of them being operative concurrently.

Early research indicates that patterns exist and change efforts must constantly be tweaked in real time as organizations plow through the pandemic to recovery. Information technology has to be embraced in both onboarding and for seasoned executives for survival to be imminent. We have found that information technology is not easily adaptable for some but with the chance for survival in a concurrent pandemic world, we found that only the people that became familiar with technology survive.

Behavior has become an elusive target as many people are not sitting by the computer all day and yet the perception is that human resources are available 24-hours a day, seven days a week. One can only suggest that based on these above conclusions that, in a post pandemic world, problems are dealt with in a remote setting leaving a time-lapse for both evaluation and application.

Technological infrastructures have to adapt accordingly and there is a considerable alignment between the knowledge-based view of the firm and information technology, and this will improve communication among remote workers if used adequately. More specifically, remote worker knowledge acquired through learning from others, subsequently posit that information technology is a strategic factor for competitive advantage in the post-COVID era. Thus, giving people platform space and presentation time is an effective used of time and resources because information technology when used as an internal resource can positively influence competitive advantage through developing platforms for remote workers.

The Transformational Leader's Vital Role

Executives are taking a serious look at all leadership ideas and suggestions today with the plethora of options available to them. Some focus on transformational leadership.

Scholars show the crucial role of transformational leadership in facilitating the knowledge acquisition process and ensuring competitive advantage in a hypercompetitive work environment. Most scholars agree that transformational leadership improves knowledge integration through enhancing knowledge sharing. Transformational leadership builds a climate that inspires followers to share knowledge in a productive and prosperous manner.

For over forty years of training executives, we found that sixty percent of an executive's time was in effect following up and tweaking strategic initiatives. This is more prevalent during the post-pandemic period. Executives spend a great deal of time conceptualizing strategic endeavors and scholars affirm that the strategic role for transformational leaders is enhanced when information technology implementation occurs at the right time and place. Thus, transformational leaders raise the levels of awareness on the importance of technology and empower people to improve information technology implementation within organizations.

When executives view Information technology as an organizational resource that facilitates organizational communications and improves the search for knowledge, they begin to see opportunities for successful business ventures. Transformational leaders enhance effectiveness when they blend technological communication to enhance their leadership role. Scholars found a significant correlation between transformational leadership and perceived usefulness of the information technology within organizations. We affirm that transformational leaders create a higher degree of technology acceptance through enabling employees to analyze problems and challenge followers to be more innovative.

Management consultants can train on the knowledge-based view. For example, in the post-COVID world, knowledge is shared via Zoom, WebEx, and internal communication systems. With some limitations, knowledge is vibrant and, in some cases, real-time. The limitations are security and hackers coupled with individually sponsored internet connections. Those organizations that managed to capitalize on information technology survived and continue to thrive today. Thus, the capability of organizations to integrate the employee's specialized knowledge into products and services can largely generate competitive advantage. This competitive advantage has prospered for some and has eliminated some of the players from the marketplace. Hence, survivors found that the information technology that reflects an internal resource that is used to manage knowledge and creates competitive advantage would thrive in the post-pandemic world. The following schematic can be the focal point of training and development.

Figure 1 provides a snapshot of how transformational leadership; information technology and knowledge management are linked.

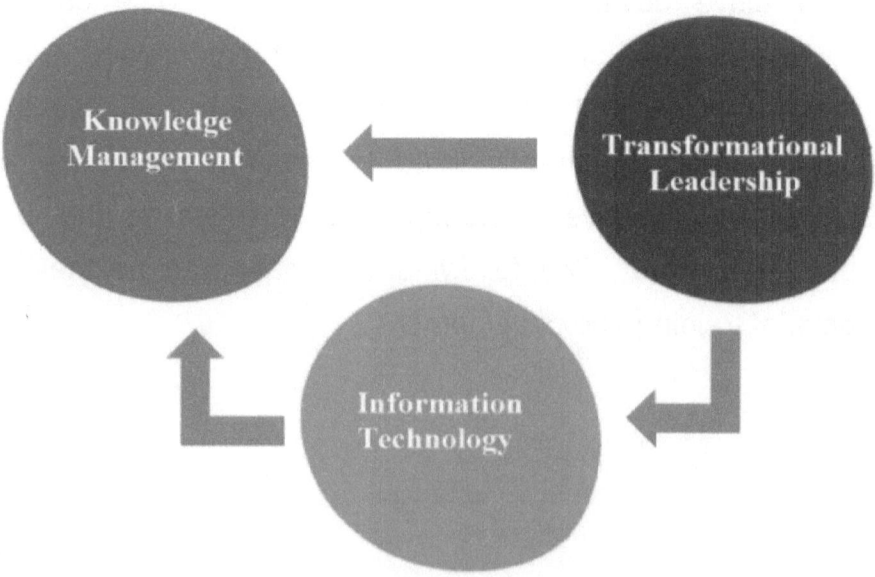

Conclusion

Transformational leadership, information technology, and knowledge management have played a significant role in recovery plans during the post-pandemic period.

The key for management consultants is that executives acting as transformational leaders can enable information technology and knowledge management as they prepare for the post-pandemic.

Without a grasp on these two tenets, executives are bound to fail in the post-pandemic. Begin to address the confines and dimensions of Transformational Leadership, then focus on developing sound information technology, and manage expertise through storing knowledge, retrieving knowledge, archiving knowledge, gathering knowledge, and hosting knowledge management.

Chapter 14

Emerging Technologies and Knowledge-based Companies

Technology, as one would imagine, is often associated with information dispersed within companies. Information technology develops and disseminates knowledge throughout the organization which, in turn, is an important factor of sustainable competitive advantage.

The effects of emerging technologies (i.e., communication and decision-aid technologies) on organizations is extending the office space to remote work and a combination of both.

What Information Technology Is

Information technology enables knowledge management by using three possible mechanisms:

- Impersonal,
- Personal, and;
- Collective.

When management consulting is helping executives use impersonal mechanism to enact regulations, procedures, and rules aimed at coordinating intellectual capital within organizations, the consultant is acting as a catalyst.

Information technology disseminates protocols among members and allows them to be knowledgeable of their progress toward meeting determined milestones stated in the strategic plans.

The personal mechanism is used by executives for the vertically and horizontally exchange of knowledge between employees and collective mechanisms. Thus, Information technology is used when it manifests itself as a synthesizer of ideas and knowledge which is acquired from multiple organizational members.

Information technology encourages people to embark on technological facilities, such as shared electronic workspaces, to provide new ideas and possible solutions for solving organizational problems. As a result, it is viewed that information technology plays a critical role in integrating knowledge within organizations.

Management consultants must be aware that executives can use information technology as a communication mechanism manifestation, for deployment of resources, and as decision-aid technology. For example, communication technology provides the ways to enhance interactions among members and departments within organizations. This type of technology eliminates the barriers of organizational communications while improving the extent of knowledge sharing and access for all followers at various levels of the organization. Thus, communication technology develops relationships within organizations to aggregate human capital into social capital so as to provide further information and opportunities for all members, and subsequently create valuable resources for an organization as a whole.

Decision-aid technology develops cohesive infrastructures to store and retrieve knowledge to enable followers in creating more innovative solutions to problems and managing operational risks. Ergo, communication and decision-aid technologies support knowledge by enabling interactions and providing more comprehensive and effective solutions to solve organizational problems.

Communication and Decision-aid Technologies

Today, technology has changed the business world ten-fold. Every day there is an easier way to process, to access, and to disseminate information. Technology, now referred to as, Information technology, is an internal resource that increasingly facilitates organizational communication and improves the search for knowledge. When executives have people in place to manage information technology, the organization can see increased revenues, better satisfaction by employees and customers, and most importantly, enhance effectiveness of leaders.

Knowledge creation is highly dependent on developing organizational communications and interactions, while

Information technology enables organizations to overcome space constraints in communication and promotes the depth and range of knowledge access and sharing within companies.

Communication technologies can be employed to enhance the conversations and knowledge exchange between organizational members. This knowledge shared through information technology could positively contribute to knowledge management.

Knowledge sharing itself can develop a more innovative climate and facilitate knowledge creation in organizations. Thus, communication technologies can play a crucial role in improving knowledge creation. Therefore, communication technology is an internal resource that develops and integrates organizational knowledge as the most strategic factor of competitiveness. To implement this technology, management consultants can help executives develop the most essential technological infrastructures to:

- Provide information technology support for collaborative work regardless of time and place, and;
- Provide information technology, support for communication among organizational employees.

Today, executives use expert systems for decision-making and technology becomes a decision-aid. Decision-aid technology can be also considered as a facilitator of the knowledge creation process through providing the essential infrastructure to store and retrieve organizational knowledge. To implement this technology, management consultants can help executives develop the most essential technological infrastructures to:

- Provide information technology support for searching for accessing necessary information, and;
- Provide information technology support for systematic storing of knowledge.

Information technology (IT) enhances learning and sharing of knowledge by providing access to knowledge. Moreover, IT stimulates new ideas and knowledge generation, transfers an individual's knowledge to other members and departments, and improves knowledge capturing, knowledge storing, and knowledge accumulating, aiming at achieving superior organizational goals.

Conclusion

Communication and decision-aid technologies have a positive association with knowledge management performance in organizations.

Many organizations still implement knowledge

management initiatives without sufficient consideration of their technological infrastructures. When executives ensure the effectiveness of knowledge management projects, they increase control and lesson operational risk. We also suggest that a firm's ability to enhance knowledge management can be highly affected when executives implement communication and decision-aid technologies.

Furthermore, we suggest that executives take these ideas and continue to meet the needs of managerial implications at the higher echelons of organizations worldwide.

Chapter 15

Driving Diversity, Equity and Inclusion

This chapter suggests new insights to identify workplace diversity as a primary driver of sales, profitability and financial performance for organizations. Management consultants will see that improving financial performance and sales requires developing diversity and inclusion within organizations---not only at the higher echelons of the organization but at every level. Dr. Provitera, in a role as member of an equity, diversity, and inclusion group at a mid-sized university in Miami, Florida, found that thinking about diversity in everything one does is important. Thus, teaching, writing, and researching about the topic, and consciously incorporating a diversity mindset at work goes along way in building an inclusive culture. Here is an excerpt, written by Dr. Mike Provitera, in his work on Diversity, Equity, and Inclusion published the following statement below.

The Anti-Racism and Equity Coalition is comprised of members from all departments across campus. The diversity of our members is meant to help us gain unique perspectives on university matters. Our goal is to ensure that the Coalition's mission permeates throughout the community. To satisfy this aim, we created the Voices of the Coalition, where Coalition members have a chance to write about their perspectives.

In this segment, we highlight the voice of member Michael Provitera, DBA, Associate Professor in the Department of Leadership Studies who discusses personal leadership prowess.

Approaching our leadership prowess? Many people feel that leaders are born and not made. Sure, leaders are born, so are preachers, doctors, lawyers, painters, and nurses, etc. The key is to do something between the time we are born and the time we leave this place, we call earth. Thus, leadership prowess is an art that needs nurturing.

Reading articles, cases, news, stories, and the classics is one way to approach our development of leadership. A great example of leadership prowess is a survivor of the holocaust. As a young teenager, Mihaly Csikszentmihalyi survived the Nazi concentration camps. In them, he felt terrible about how so many people died. He noticed that a few people, despite the horrible conditions, survived. He later came to the United States, studied psychology, became department chair at the University of Chicago, and spent his career investigating this phenomenon of the few that survived the holocaust. Over time, he named his thesis "Flow." Flow, he said, is a collection of phenomena with unknown beginnings and ends. People can experience flow when they are doing something that they enjoy. They begin feeling a sense of self-efficacy. Our personal leadership prowess is our unique special character. Thus, go with the flow.

The global approach to management consulting represents and requires an effective and efficient process to train executives to adapt to various environments successfully. Culture has always been important, and today, developing the most appropriate culture to help everyone thrive is essential. Executives can contribute to the dynamic market needs, through adopting a diversity, equity, and inclusion strategy.

Our first training begins with a deep dive into diversity to create a sense of awareness of the executive mindset toward diversity, equity, and inclusion. This is leadership development in diversity, equity, and inclusion at its best because it allows participants to be authentic leaders. The roots come from our upbringing, our training, and the people that have influenced us since childhood. For those who may remember the trainings that helped people develop a unique sense of wellbeing in the 80s and 90s that were very popular.

Here is the one program that I am comparing to the deep dive training in diversity, equity, and inclusion:

> Erhard Seminars Training (marketed as **Est**, though often encountered as EST or Est) was an organization, founded by Werner Erhard in 1971, that offered a three-weekend (6-day, 60-hour) course known officially as "The Est Standard Training." The seminar aimed to transform one's ability to experience living so that the situations that one had been trying to change or had been dealing with, at this point in their life, clear up just in the process of life itself. An **Est** website claims that the training brought to the forefront the ideas of transformation, personal responsibility, accountability, and possibility." Est seminars operated from late 1971 to late 1984 and spawned a number of books from 1976 to 2011. Est has been featured in a number of films and television shows. Est represented an outgrowth of the Human Potential Movement] of the 1960s through to the 1970s.

Similar to EST, diversity, equity, and inclusion in the workplace plays a critical role and is a strategic prerequisite for business success in today's hypercompetitive global environment. In particular, a diversity, equity, and inclusion strategy can help organizations to improve financial performance in terms of achieving commercial goals and the develop the best quality of products and services.

As management consultants, we realize that the ultimate business outcome is financial success that is achieved both honestly and ethically, which by far, narrows the gap between not only success and failure, but also, survival. However, financial success is only achieved by the commitment of its members and facilitated by executives that promote diversity, equity, and inclusion. Survival alone helps people maintaining their career and livelihood. Thus, there is a corollary between financial success and employee success and one way to meet this corollary is by accepting and implementing a diversity, equity, and diversity platform.

Management consultants can help executives focus on the critical human assets which represent human capital and can lead to a stronger core competence. By developing follower attitudes and values to accomplish a higher degree of effectiveness, executives can highlight the importance of employees in implementing changes at the organizational level.

By showing concern for the employee's individual needs and accepting people for who they are, employees begin to contribute more toward organizational goals, they feel more commitment to their career, and they become more inspired. Thus, diversity, equity, and inclusion, results in higher human capital, in which employees put in extra effort and improves the quality of products and customer satisfaction. Focusing on human capital impacts the return on assets, sales, shareholder value, and improves financial success and operational risk management.

Diversity, equity, and inclusion incorporates strategic endeavors that enhance the human capital and social capital as the culture becomes more fluid for employees. Fluidity in cultural prowess using diversity, equity, and inclusive skills coupled with strong interpersonal relations that is based on trust and reciprocity can improve innovation and the performance of group cohesiveness.

With an effective diversity, equity, and inclusion strategy, executives can improve knowledge sharing and learning that can eventually enhance financial performance in global markets through empowering human resources and enabling change at the organizational level.

Management consultants can help executives increase workplace diversity, equity, and inclusion and facilitate knowledge sharing by building relationships, and aiming at improving customer satisfaction through training on the soft skills necessary for personal development. By continuously acquiring additional knowledge from customers and developing better relationships with them, organizations can provide a higher quality of service and products for them. Organizations are just beginning to realize, in 2022, that building a diverse, equity, and inclusion type of workplace meets the needs of the people that buy their products and services and they become organizational advocates of their brand.

Leadership must create a team or steering committee that makes diversity, equity, and inclusion a priority and represents a variety of ideas and perspectives of all organizational members. Giving voice and recognition to all employees.

Conclusion

The fact remains that management consultants that help executives manage diversity, equity, and inclusion use it as an important driving force for financial success and customer satisfaction. The organizations that embrace diversity, equity, and inclusion are more competitive and on the cutting edge of employee development. In a recent publication called ***Founders Mag: Entrepreneurial Insight for Success***, Dr. Provitera posited the following leadership characteristic of the future:

> *By far the biggest leadership skill to have today is diversity, equity, and inclusion. Leaders need this skill, and they will hire the people that have diversity, equity, and inclusion skills. They will need to know what to look*

for in their followers, how to plan a culture of acceptance, and how to strategize in a diversified playing field. Not only are the clients that buy the organization's products and services interested in how the organization accepts diversity, equity, and inclusion, but also, the future talent that want to work there will investigate the organization's ability to address diversity, equity, and inclusion.

When companies can have a very diverse employee population, they will secure a foothold in the ever-expansive global business environment.

Chapter 16

Talent Management

The double edge sword of management consultant is built on the foundation of talent management. Talent management is both an external concern as the management consultant attracts clientele and an internal concern as consultants continuously develop content for training and consulting. Thus, knowing and addressing talent management is tantamount to success. Formulate these six pillars of success into your practice and build your management consulting black box.

1. Prioritize Candidate Experience

Instilling knowledge in others is a collection of meaningful experiences. By prioritizing candidate experience, the consultant can enable organizations to solve problems and create value through improved performance. The key here is to narrow the gaps of success and failure leading to more successful decision-making. Help people help themselves through coaching and mentoring them.

2. Tailor Talent Management Strategy to Business Goals

Consultants must focus on the day-to-day operations, but success is based upon helping executives determine business goals for both the short- and long-term. The key is based upon planning the work and technically supporting talented individuals to achieve both personal and professional goals. Promoting some kind of higher order of effectiveness attracts both the clients and participants. Some clients may create steering committees that drive decision making and these teams need specific training tailored to their needs. The no-jerk policy must be adhered to so that employees feel they are free of criticism at work. Organizations have a low tolerance for jerks.

3. Educate the Hiring Manager

As management consultants, we are always teaching. By becoming familiar with the employee recruitment practices, the consultant can become better educators. Educating participants is more active, broader, and more flexible compared to training sophisticated content. There is also the adherence to disabled and less fortunate employees. Organizations must cater to this group to ensure equitable working conditions for all.

4. Enhancing Training Efficiency

Training is an effective way to share knowledge. The words "share-knowledge" is important because the trainer that works off the sentiment of the room can quickly adapt to participant needs. From the onset of a training, a gap analysis, which is an identification of key concepts to be addressed, and then tailoring the training to those needs is most appropriate. To provide better decision-making and work-related practices, questions such as what is happening in business today at your organization, what would you like to learn about the subject are written down and then at the end of the training, circled back, checked off, or re-addressed if left out or in need of more attention.

Building a foundation creates new knowledge through innovation and implementation.

Thomas Edison, the great inventor, followed many processes to capture knowledge, innovation, and implementation. Try to get the participants to think like Edison did and organizations will be more innovative and creative.

Here is Thomas Edison's recipe for success:

1) Use Primary Resources
2) Develop questions for Analyzing Primary Sources
3) Create critical Analysis Written Document Sheet
4) Build a photo Analysis Worksheet
5) Create a poster Analysis Worksheet
6) Create a political Cartoon Analysis Sheet
7) Think Like a Historian (Source: New Jersey Digital Highway)

When thinking like a historian, knowledge has to be measured in some way, many trainers talk about return-on-investment of the training which is hard to measure. While return on investment may be tacitly built into training and development as people get promoted and utilize the skills taught during training, this is not always measured. Training satisfaction measurement by participants and their desire to apply concepts to the workplace is an excellent barometer of learning new skills or building upon old ones. This can be captured at the end of the training session directly from participants and this holds much value. For example, after being trained in a four hour deep-dive Equity, Diversity, and Inclusion training, Dr. Mike, the author of this book, felt the need to immediately implement the same training to anyone and everyone at the same organization. Thus, quickly applying what is taught or learned is the best way to develop the skills of management consulting and training.

5. Innovative Services

Management consultants can motivate employees to approach organizational problems in more novel ways. New and different applications of knowledge that have never been done before places organizations ahead of the competition. Inspiring employees to rethink problems and challenges in new ways coupled with their current personal attitudes and values to help them become self-aware of their personal and professional limitations is a large part of Authentic Leadership.

Consultants attempt to change the basic values, beliefs, and attitudes of employees so that they are willing to perform beyond their previous, or original level, before the training. Jim Clawson captured this mindset in his book titled "Level Three Leadership: How to Become an Effective Executive," published by Business Expert Press, and edited by Dr. Michael Provitera. Jim emphasizes that leading from the heart and mind as opposed to leading from the pressure of rewards and punishment is the way to create buy-in from followers. Jim's Level Three Leadership is a worldwide acknowledged and accepted approach to executive leadership training.

By training on the three levels: Visible Behavior, Conscious Thought, and semi-conscious VABES (Values, Assumptions, Beliefs, and Expectations of how the world is and how it is expected to be), participants and executives can understand authentic leadership and provide innovative services.

6. Flexibility

Building a flexible platform for training by working off the participant's needs, and their current events is important. The same with flexibility in the workplace which may enable companies to improve departmental and managerial interactions and develop relationships among managers, business units, and departments, by employing diversity, equity, and inclusive skills.

Through flexibility in the workplace, consultants can

help executives shift the power of decision-making to the lower levels and inspire newly hired employees to create new ideas and implement them, which can in turn propel interdepartmental communications and improve knowledge exchange. At Morgan Stanley, an investment bank in Manhattan, New York, Dr. Provitera requested to join the CEO in his "breakfast with the CEO" meetings that were voluntary. These meetings turned out to be fruitful with new ideas and prospects based on a simple breakfast discussion between the upper echelon executives and employees.

Another example in in South Florida, at an organization called Assurant Solutions. Kurt Landon created a new version of a suggestion box. Kurt requested that he needed to see any suggestion that was turned down by a manager or supervisor before it was not addressed.

Conclusion

Talent management is the cornerstone of management consulting. The focus must be on continuous personal development for oneself, then the staff of the consulting organization, and finally for the client. One cannot develop the client if one does not develop oneself.

Continuous improvement is the secret ingredient in the management consultant's black box.

Each week, take an hour on Sunday night to reflect on what you accomplished during the week and what you want to address in the coming week. Each month, take a weekend to celebrate and reflect on your success. Each year, take a week to celebrate your successes, reflect on your experience, and plan the next year accordingly.

References

Chapter 1

1. Balogun, J. and Jenkins, M. (2003). Re-conceiving Change Management: A Knowledge-based Perspective. European Management Journal, 21(2), 247-257.
2. Cardinal, L.B. (2001). Technological innovation in the pharmaceutical industry: the use of organizational control in managing research and development. Organization Science, 12(1), 19-36.
3. Damanpour, F. (1991). Organizational innovation: A meta-analysis of effects of determinants and moderators. Academy of Management Journal, 34(3), 555–590.
4. Garvin, D.A. (1993). Building a learning organization. Harvard Business Review, 71(4), 78–91.
5. Huber, G.P. (1991). Organizational learning: The contributing process and the literatures. Organization Science, 2(1), 88–115.
6. Jung, D., Wu, A. and Chow, C.W. (2008). Towards understanding the direct and indirect effects of CEOs'

transformational leadership on firm innovation. The Leadership Quarterly, 19(5), 582-594.

7. Sivadas, E. and Dwyer, F.R. (2000). An examination of organizational factors influencing new product success in internal and alliance-based processes. Journal of Marketing, 64(1), 31–50.

8. Woodman, R.W., Sawyer, J.E. and Griffin, R.W. (1993). Toward a theory of organizational creativity. Academy of Management Review, 18(2), 293-321.

9. Provitera, M. J. & Sayyadi, M. (2022). "Teaching and Learning Styles in Management Education with a Focus on Transformational Leadership,' JOURNAL OF BUSINESS, & LEADERSHIPSCHOOL OF BUSINESS AND TECHNOLOGY, VOL. 4 (1): Winter, 2022: 1-15.

10. Todd Henshaw, PhD, Senior Fellow, Center for Leadership and Change Management, The Wharton School; former Director of Military Leadership, West Point. Found on March 3, 2022 on website: https://executiveeducation.wharton.upenn.edu/wp-content/uploads/2021/06/NanoTool-2021-07.pdf

11. IBIS World, Where Knowledge is Power, September 29, 2021. Found on March 3, 2022 on website: https://www.ibisworld.com/industry-statistics/employment/management-consulting-united-states/

12. Van de Ven, A. (1986). Central Problems in the Management of Innovation, Management Science Vol. 32, No. 5

13 Executive Job Demands: New Insights for Explaining

Strategic Decisions and Leader Behaviors

July 2005The Academy of Management Review 30(3):472-491 Journal

DOI: 10.5465/AMR.2005.17293355

Donald C. Hambrick, Sydney Finkelstein. Ann C. Mooney

Chapter 2

1. Avolio, B.J., Waldman, D.A., & Yammarino, F.J. (1991). Leading in the 1990s: the four I's of transformational leadership. Journal of European Industrial Training, 15(4), 9-16.
2. Canty, L.T. (2005). Conceptual assessment: transformational, transactional and laissez-faire leadership styles and job performances of managers as perceived by their direct reports [Unpublished doctoral dissertation]. Capella University.
3. Cardinal, L.B. (2001). Technological innovation in the pharmaceutical industry: the use of organizational control in managing research and development. Organization Science, 12 (1), 19-36.
4. Horwitz, I.B., Horwitz, S.K., Daram, P., Brandt, M.L., Brunicardi, F.C., & Awad, S.S. (2008). Transformational, transactional, and passive-avoidant leadership characteristics of a surgical resident cohort: analysis using the multifactor leadership questionnaire

and implications for improving surgical education curriculums. The Journal of surgical research, 148(1), 49-59.

5. Marr, B., Gupta, O., Roos, G., & Pike, S. (2003). Intellectual capital and knowledge management effectiveness. Management Decision, 41(8), 771-781.

6. Neeley, T. (2021). Remote Work Revolution: Succeeding from Anywhere. New York: HarperCollins Publishers LLC.

7. Patiar, A., & Mia, L. (2009). Transformational leadership style, market competition and departmental performance: Evidence from luxury hotels in Australia. International Journal of Hospitality Management, 28(2), 254-262.

8. Sivadas, E., & Dwyer, F.R. (2000). An examination of organizational factors influencing new product success in internal and alliance-based processes. Journal of Marketing, 64(1), 31–50.

9. Wenger, E.C. (1998). Communities of practice. London: Cambridge University Press.

10. Zheng, W., Yang, B., & Mclean, G.N. (2010). Linking organizational culture, structure, strategy, and organizational effectiveness: mediating role of knowledge management. Journal of Business Research, 63(7), 763-771.

11. Argyris, C (1960) Understanding Organizational Behavior. Homewood, IU.: Dorsey Press.

Chapter 3

1. Barney, J.B. (1991), "Firm Resources and Sustained Competitive Advantage", Journal of Management, Vol. 17, No. 1, pp. 99-120.
2. Bass, B.M. and Avolio, B.J. (1997), Full range leadership development: Manual for the Multifactor Leadership Questionnaire, MindGarden, California.
3. Bennis, W. and Nanus, B. (1985). Leaders: The strategies for taking charge, Harper, New York.
4. Canty, L.T. (2005), "Conceptual assessment: Transformational, transactional and laissez-faire leadership styles and job performances of managers as perceived by their direct reports", Capella University, USA.
5. Eagly, A.H. and Carli, L.L. (2003), "The female leadership advantage: An evaluation of the evidence", The Leadership Quarterly, Vol. 14, No. 6, pp. 807-834.
6. Jung, D., Wu, A. and Chow, C.W. (2008), "Towards understanding the direct and indirect effects of CEOs' transformational leadership on firm innovation", The Leadership Quarterly, Vol. 19, No. 5, pp. 582-594.

7. Purvis, R.L., Sambamurthy, V. and Zmud R.W. (2000), "The development of knowledge embeddedness in CASE technologies within organizations", IEEE Transactions on Engineering Management, Vol. 47, No. 2, pp. 245-257.
8. Venkatraman, N. (1989), "Strategic orientation of business enterprises: the construct, dimensionality, and measurement", Management Science, Vol. 35, No. 8, pp. 942-962.
9. Zheng, W. (2005), "The impact of organizational culture, structure, and strategy on knowledge management effectiveness and organizational effectiveness", University of Minnesota, USA.
10. Zheng, W., Yang, B. and Mclean, G.N. (2010), "Linking organizational culture, structure, strategy, and organizational effectiveness: Mediating role of knowledge management", Journal of Business Research, Vol. 63, No. 7, pp. 763-771.
11. Moldoveanu, M and Narayandas, D. (2019) The Future of Leadership Development: Gaps in traditional executive education are creating room for approaches that are more tailored and democratic. Harvard Business Review (March–April 2019):

Chapter 4

1. AESC (2020), The Future of Executive Search and Leadership Consulting, Executive Talent, 17, pp. 4-15.
2. Burns, J.M. (1978) Leadership, Harper & Row, New York.
3. Eagly, A.H., & Carli, L.L. (2003). The female leadership advantage: An evaluation of the evidence. The Leadership Quarterly, 14(6), 807-834.
4. Patiar, A., & Mia, L. (2009). Transformational leadership style, market competition and departmental performance: Evidence from luxury hotels in Australia. International Journal of Hospitality Management, 28(2), 254-262.
5. Yukl, G & Van Fleet, DD (1992) Theory and research on leadership in organizations. In Dunnette MD & Hough LM (eds), Handbook of Industrial and Organizational Psychology, vol. 3, pp. 147-197, Consulting Psychologists Press, Palo Alto, CA.
6. Van de Ven, A. (2017). *Managing Knowledge Integration Across Boundaries*, Oxford University Press.

Chapter 5

1. Bennis, W 2009, On Becoming a Leader, Basic Books, New York.

2. George, B 2003, Authentic leadership: rediscovering the secrets to creating lasting value, Jossey-Bass, San Francisco, CA.
3. Hmieleski KM, Cole MS, Baron RA 2012, Shared authentic leadership and new venture performance, Journal of Management, 38, 1476-1499
4. Markham, SE 2012, The evolution of organizations and leadership from the ancient world to modernity: A multilevel approach to organizational science and leadership, The Leadership Quarterly, 23(6), 1134-1151.
5. Mills, DQ 2005, Leadership: How to Lead, How to Live, MindEdge Press, Waltham, MA.
6. Mintzberg, H 2007, Mintzberg on Management, Free Press, New York.
7. Rost, JC 1991, Leadership for the twenty-first century, Praeger, New York.

Chapter 6

1. Campbell, A.H. (2018), Global Leadership Initiatives for Conflict Resolution and Peacebuilding, Hershey, PA: IGI Global.
2. Ibarra, H., and Scoular, A. (2019), The Leader as Coach, Harvard Business Review (November–December 2019).

3. Greenleaf, R.K. (1977), Servant Leadership: A Journey Into the Nature of Legitimate Power and Greatness, Nahwah, NJ: Paulist Press.
4. Hesse, H. (1932), The Journey to the East: A Novel. New York, NY: Picadorusa.
5. Verdorfer, A.P. (2019), The paradox of serving: Can genuine servant leadership gain followers' respect for the leader: Evidence from Germany and Lithuania, German Journal of Human Resource Management, Vol. 33, No. 2, pp. 113-136.
6. Lewis, D.E. (2019), Old Testament View of Robert Greenleaf's Servant Leadership, Journal of Biblical Perspectives in Leadership, Vol. 9, No. 1, pp. 304-318.
7. Gandolfi, F., and Stone, S. (2018), Leadership, Leadership Styles, and Servant Leadership, Journal of Management Research, Vol. 18, No. 4, pp. 261-269.
8. Lawrence, M., and Spears, L.C. (2004), Practicing Servant Leadership: Succeeding through Trust, Bravery, and Forgiveness, San Francisco: Jossey-Bass.
9. Liu, H. (2017), Just the Servant: An Intersectional Critique of Servant Leadership, Journal of Business Ethics, Vol. 156, pp. 1099-1112.

10. Scott, K.D., Callahan, J.S., and Kiker, M.B. (2019), Exploring the Boundaries of Servant Leadership: A Meta-Analysis of the Main and Moderating Effects of Servant Leadership on Behavioral and Affective Outcomes, Journal of Managerial Issues, Vol. 31, No. 2, pp. 172-197.

Chapter 8

1. Fahey, L & Prusak, L 1998 'The eleven deadliest sins of knowledge management', California Management Review, vol. 40, no. 3, p. 265-276.
2. Lee, H & Choi B 2003 'Knowledge management enablers, processes, and organizational performance: an integrative view and empirical examination', Journal of Management Information Systems, vol. 20, no. 1, pp. 179-228.
3. Leonard, D 1995, Wellsprings of knowledge: Building and sustaining the source of innovation. Harvard Business School Press, Boston, MA.
4. Leonard, D & Sensiper, S 1998 'The role of tacit knowledge in group innovation', California Management Review, vol. 40, no. 3, pp. 112–132.
5. Lines, R, Selart, M, Espedal, B & Johansen, ST 2005 'The production of trust during organizational change', Journal of Change Management, vol. 5, no. 2, pp. 221–245.

6. Ogbonna, E & Harris, L 2002 'Managing organizational culture: Insights from the hospitality industry', Human Resource journal, vol. 12, no. 1, pp. 33–53.
7. Ouchi, W & Wilkins, A 1985 'Organizational culture', Annual Review of Sociology, vol. 11, pp. 457-483.
8. Schein, E 1984 'Coming to a new awareness of organizational culture', Sloan Management Review, vol. 25, no. 2. pp. 37-50.
9. Scott, WR 2003, Organizations: Rational, nature, and open systems, Prentice Hall, Upper Saddle River, NJ.
10. Smircich, L 1983 'Concepts of culture and organizational analysis', Administrative Science Quarterly, vol. 28, no. 3, pp. 339-358.
11. Van Den Berg, PT & Wilderom, CPM 2004 'Defining, measuring, and comparing organizational cultures', Applied Psychology: An International Review, vol. 53, no. 4, pp. 570-582.
12. Washington, M.L. (2008). It's whom you know and what you know: A social capital perspective of the effect of small firm organizational learning on firm performance (Unpublished doctoral dissertation). Temple University, USA.

Chapter 10

1. Andrew, K. (1971). The Concept of Corporate Strategy. Homewood, Illinois: Irwin.
2. Bergeron, F., Raymond, L., & Rivard, S. (2004). Ideal patterns of strategic alignment and business performance. Information & management, 41 (8), 1003-1020.
3. Gilbert, A.H., & Reid, R.C. (2009). An Analysis of the Relationships among Information Scope, Organizational Proactiveness, and Firm Performance. Academy of Accounting and Financial Studies Journal, 13(4), 1-19.
4. Hofer, CW & Schendel, D. (1978). Strategy Formulation: Analytical Concepts. Saint Paul: West Publishing Company,
5. Karabulut, A.T. (2015). Effects of Innovation Strategy on Firm Performance: A Study Conducted on Manufacturing Firms in Turkey. Procedia - Social and Behavioral Sciences, 195, 1338-1347.
6. Kazaz, A., & Ulubeyli, S. (2009). Strategic management practices in Turkish construction firms. Journal of Management in Engineering, 25(4), 185-194.
7. Morgan, R.E., & Strong C.A. (2003). Business Performance and Dimensions of Strategic Orientation. Journal of Business Research, 56(3), 163-176.
8. Rumelt, R.P. (1979). Evaluation of Strategy: Theory and Models'. In D. Schendel & C.W. Hofer, (Eds.),

Strategic Management: A New View of Business Policy and Planning, Boston, MA: Little Brown.
9. Talke, K. (2007). Corporate mindset of innovating firms: Influences on new product performance. Journal of Engineering and Technology Management, 24, 76-91.
10. Venkatraman, N. (1989). Strategic orientation of business enterprises: the construct, dimensionality, and measurement. Management Science, 35(8), 942-962.
11. Zheng, W. (2005). The impact of organizational culture, structure, and strategy on knowledge management effectiveness and organizational effectiveness (Unpublished doctoral dissertation). University of Minnesota, USA.
12. Zheng, W., Yang, B., & Mclean, G.N. (2010). Linking organizational culture, structure, strategy, and organizational effectiveness: Mediating role of knowledge management. Journal of Business Research, 63(7), 763-771.

Chapter 11

1. Demarest, M. (1997). Understanding knowledge management. Long Range Planning, 30(3), 374-384.
2. Long, D.W.D., & Fahey, L. (2000). Diagnosing cultural barriers to knowledge management. The Academy of Management Executive, 14(4), 113-127.

3. Lee, J.H., & Kim, Y.G. (2001). A stage model of organizational knowledge management: a latent content analysis. Expert Systems with Applications, 20(4), 299-311.
4. Jianbin, C., Yanli, G., & Kaibo, X. (2014). Value Added from Knowledge Collaboration: Convergence of Intellectual Capital and Social Capital. International Journal of u- and e- Service, Science and Technology, 7(2),.15-26.
5. Zehua, Z. (2012). Knowledge Collaboration (KC) and the relationship between KC and some related concepts. Library and Information Service, 8, 107–112.

Chapter 12

1. Alavi, M., & Leidner, D.E. (2001). Review: Knowledge Management and Knowledge Management Systems: Conceptual Foundations and Research Issues. MIS Quarterly, 25(1), 107-136.
2. Amidon, D.M. (1997). Innovation strategy for the knowledge economy. Boston, MA: Butterworth-Heinemann.
3. Argote, L., & Ingram, P. (2000). Knowledge transfer: A Basis for Competitive Advantage in Firms.

Organizational Behavior and Human Decision Processes, 82(1), 150–169.
4. Award, E.M., & Ghaziri, H.M. (2004). Knowledge Management, Upper Saddle River, NJ: Prentice Hall.
5. Beckman, T.J. (1999). The Current State of Knowledge Management. In J. Liebowitz, (Eds.), Knowledge Management Handbook, New York: CRC Press.
6. Bell, D. (1999). The axial age of technology foreword: 1999. In B. Smart, (Eds.), The Coming of the Post-Industrial Society. New York: Basic Books.
7. Bock, G. (2001). Determinants of the Individual's Knowledge Sharing Behavior in the Organization: The Theory of Reasoned Action Perspective (Unpublished doctoral dissertation). Korea Advanced Institute of Science and Technology, South Korea.
8. Drucker, P. (1998). The future that has already happened. The Futurist, 32(8), 16-18.
9. Grover, V., Davenport, T.H. (2001). General Perspectives on Knowledge Management: Fostering a Research Agenda. Journal of Management Information Systems, 18(1), 5-21.
10. Lee, J.H., & Kim, Y.G. (2001). A stage model of organizational knowledge management: a latent content analysis. Expert Systems with Applications, 20(4), 299-311.
11. Ruggles, R.L. (1997). Knowledge management tools, Boston, MA: Butterworth-Heinemann.

12. Senge, P.M. (1997). Communities of leaders and learners. Harvard Business Review, 75(5), 30-32.
13. Truch E. (2001). Knowledge management: Auditing and Reporting Intellectual Capital. Journal of General Management, 26(3), 26-40.
14. Tsoukas, H., & Vladimirou, E. (2001). What is Organizational Knowledge? Journal of Management Studies, 38 (7), 973-993.
15. Wiig, K.M. (1993). Knowledge Management Foundations: Thinking About Thinking – How People and Organizations Create, Represent, and Use Knowledge. Arlington, Texas: Schema Press.
16. Wiseman, E. (2008). The institutionalization of organizational knowledge: Learning to walk the talk (Unpublished doctoral dissertation). McGill University, Canada.

Chapter 13

1. Aulakh, P.S., Kundu, S.K., & Lahiri, S. (2016). Learning and knowledge management in and out of emerging markets: Introduction to the special issue. 51(5), 655-661.
2. Curado, C. (2006). The knowledge-based view of the firm: from theoretical origins to future implications.

Retrieved from http://citeseerx.ist.psu.edu/viewdoc/download?doi=10.1.1.322.8178&rep=rep1&type=pdf.
3. De Carolis, D. (2002). The Role of Social Capital and Organizational Knowledge in Enhancing Entrepreneurial Opportunities in High-Technology Environments, In Choo & Bontis (Eds.), The Strategic Management of Intellectual Capital and Organizational Knowledge, New York: Oxford University Press.
4. Dorfler, V. (2010). Learning capability: the effect of existing knowledge on learning. Knowledge Management Research & Practice, 8, 369–379.
5. Eisenhardt, K., & Santos, F. (2006). Knowledge-based view: A new theory of strategy? In H. Pettigrew, & T.R. Whittington (Eds.), Handbook of strategy and management, London: Sage Publications Ltd.
6. Hu, J., Huang, K-T., Kuse, J., Su, GW., & Wang, K.Y. (1997). Customer Information Quality and Knowledge Management: A Case Study Using Knowledge Cockpit. Journal of Knowledge Management, 1(3), 225-236
7. Keskin, H. (2005). The Relationships Between Explicit and Tacit Oriented KM Strategy, and Firm Performance. Journal of American Academy of Business, Cambridge, 7(1), 169-175.
8. Kogut, B., & Zander, U. (1993). Knowledge of the firm and the evolutionary theory of the multinational corporation. Journal of International Business Studies, 24(4), 625-645.

9. Kogut, B., & Zander, U. (1992). Knowledge of the firm, combinative capabilities, and the replication of technology. Organization Science, 3, 383-397.
10. Linderman, K., Schoeder, R.G., Zaheer, S., Liedtke, C., & Choo, A.S. (2004). Integrating quality management practices with knowledge creation processes. Journal of Operations Management, 22(6), 589-607.
11. Matusik, S.F. (1998). The Utilization of Contingent Work, Knowledge Creation, and Competitive Advantage. The Academy of Management Review, 23(4), 680-697.
12. North K., Reinhardt, R., & Schmidt A. (2004). The Benefits of Knowledge Management: Some empirical evidence. v Retrieved from http://www2.warwick.ac.uk/fac/soc/wbs/ conf/olkc/archive /oklc5/papers/a-8_north.pdf.
13. Spender, J.C. (1996). Organizational knowledge, learning and memory: three concepts in search of a theory. Journal of Organizational Change Management, 9(1), 63-78.
14. Sukumaran, S., Sukumaran, S., Shetty, M.V., & Shetty, M.V. (2009). Knowledge Management (KM) in automobile: Application of a value chain (VC) approach using KM tools, Retrieved from http://ieeexplore.ieee.org/stamp/stamp.jsp?arnumber=0 54025 54.

Chapter 14

1. Avila Cobo, SH 2005, Collaboration, innovation and the building blocks of social capital in the technology sector: A comparative analysis of knowledge-creating institutions. The role of individual attributes, policies and environments in the collaboration and productivity of scientists and technologists, Thesis, Stanford, Stanford University.

2. Choi, B 2002) Knowledge Management Enablers, Processes, and Organizational Performance: An Integration and Empirical Examination, Thesis, Daejeon, Korea Advanced Institute of Science and Technology.

3. Claudia, S, Brock, SJ, & Shaw, E 2017, 'Embracing digital networks: Entrepreneurs' social capital online', Journal of Business Venturing, Elsevier, vol. 32, no. 1, pp. 18-34.

4. Coleman, JS 1988, 'Social Capital in the Creation of Human Capital', The American Journal of Sociology, vol. 94, no. 1, pp. 95-120.

5. Cots, EG 2011, 'Stakeholder social capital: a new approach to stakeholder theory', Business Ethics: A European Review, vol. 20, no. 4, pp. 328-341.

6. Lyonga, EN 2017, Risks Management Application in Helping the Poor Through Microfinancing, Thesis, Minnesota Walden University.

7. Nahapiet, J, & Ghoshal, S 1998, 'Social Capital, Intellectual Capital, and the Organizational Advantage', The Academy of Management Review, vol. 23, no. 2, pp. 242-266.

8. Ostrom, E, & Ahn, TK 2003, 'Introduction', in E Ostrom, & TK Ahn (ed.), Foundations of Social Capital, Edward Elgar Publishing, Cheltenham, pp. xi-xxxix.

9. Putnam, RD 2000, Bowling alone: the collapse and revival of American community, Simon & Schuster, New York.

10. Putnam, RD, Leonardi, R, & Nanetti, R 1993, Making democracy work: civic traditions in modern Italy, Princeton University Press, Princeton.

11. Schein, EH 1985, Organizational culture and leadership, Jossey-Bass Publishers, San Francisco.

12. Villalonga-Olives, E & Kawachi, I 2015, 'The measurement of social capital', Gaceta Sanitaria, vol. 29, no. 1, pp. 62-64.

13. Wang, CL, & Ahmed, PK 2003, 'Structure and structural dimensions for knowledge-based organizations', Measuring Business Excellence, vol. 7, no. 1, pp. 51-62.

Chapter 15

1. Birasnav, M. (2014). Knowledge management and organizational performance in the service industry: The role of transformational leadership beyond the effects of transactional leadership. Journal of Business Research, Vol. 67, No. 8, pp. 1622-1629.
2. Darroch, J. (2005). Knowledge management, innovation and firm performance. Journal of Knowledge Management, 9(3), 101 – 115.
3. Eom, M., Kahai, S., & Yayla, A. (2015). Investigation of How IT Leadership Impacts IT-Business Alignment through Shared Domain Knowledge and knowledge Integration. https://pdfs.semanticscholar.org/c150/38187023e0d3fc53da1fdf359f5d1386352d.pdf
4. Noseworthy, S. (1998). "Transformational leadership and information technology: implications for secondary school Leaders" PhD Thesis. Memorial University of Newfoundland, Canada.
5. Lin, R.S., & Hsiao, J.K. (2014). The Relationships between Transformational Leadership, Knowledge Sharing, Trust and Organizational Citizenship Behavior. International Journal of Innovation, Management and Technology, Vol. 5, No. 3, pp. 171-174.

6. Liu, Y., & Phillips, J.S. (2011). Examining the antecedents of knowledge sharing in facilitating team innovativeness from a multilevel perspective. International Journal of Information Management, Vol. 31, No. 1, pp. 44-52
7. Politis, J. D. (2001). The relationship of various leadership styles on knowledge management. Leadership & Organizational Development Journal, Vol. 22, No. 7/8, pp. 354- 365
8. Reus, T.H. (2004). A knowledge-based view of international acquisition performance (Unpublished PhD Thesis). The Florida State University.
9. Schepers, J., Wetzels, M., & de Ruyter, K. (2005). Leadership styles in technology acceptance. Journal of Managing Service Quality, Vol. 15, No. 6, pp. 496-508.
10. Wu, I.L. and Chen J.L. (2014). Knowledge management driven firm performance: the roles of business process capabilities and organizational learning. Journal of Knowledge Management, 18(6), 1141 – 1164.
11. Yee, D. (2000). Images of school principals' information and communications technology leadership. Journal of Information Technology for teacher Education, Vol. 9, No. 3, pp. 287-302.
12. Zheng, W. (2005). The impact of organizational culture, structure, and strategy on knowledge management

effectiveness and organizational effectiveness (Unpublished PhD Thesis). University of Minnesota.

13. Zheng, W., Yang, B. and Mclean, G.N. (2010). Linking organizational culture, structure, strategy, and organizational effectiveness: Mediating role of knowledge management. Journal of Business Research, 63(7), 763-771.

Bibliography

1. Edison, T. (1884-1931). Thomas Edison and The Process of Invention. Found on website https://njdigitalhighway.org/lesson/thomas_edison on August 30, 2022.

Testimonial

I have had the honor and privilege to take a few classes with Dr. Michael Provitera under the Organizational Leadership degree at Barry University, Miami, Florida, USA. During my schooling years at Barry University and after obtaining two degrees and having many professors over this time, there is one professor I still fondly remember many years later. Dr. Michael Provitera was an inspiration, a true leader, a professor with a vision of a better future. He taught us to be the best we all can be. Dr. and Professor Michael Provitera prepared me for a life in Europe, where I have been continuing my higher education. Dr. and Professor Michael Provitera has been my inspiration in my professional career. I highly recommend that any future students that have an opportunity to learn from Dr. Provitera to embrace it.

Danilo Dominguez (They/Them), Psychologist-Systemic Psychotherapist and Counsellor. Barcelona & Zurich, written with consent to publish on December 5, 2022.

ABOUT THE AUTHORS

Dr. Michael J. Provitera, Doctor of Business Administration, is an Associate Professor of Organizational Behavior in the D. Inez Andreas School of Business and Public Administration at Barry University, Miami, Florida, USA. Michael published over 100 articles on a variety of topics in the management and leadership field and has conducted research and executive training sessions on many management issues, including executive leadership, emotional intelligence, motivation, leading change, strategic management, and management education.

Mostafa Sayyadi, CAHRI, AFAIM, CPMgr, works with senior business leaders to effectively develop innovation in companies and helps companies—from start-ups to the Fortune 100—succeed by improving the effectiveness of their leaders. Mostafa Sayyadi is an opinion columnist for the CEOWORLD magazine.

***

www.ingramcontent.com/pod-product-compliance
Lightning Source LLC
Chambersburg PA
CBHW031622210526
45464CB00004B/1705